Inerrancy and Common Sense

Inerrancy and Common Sense

EDITED BY
ROGER R. NICOLE &
J. RAMSEY MICHAELS

Contributors

John J. Davis — *Roger R. Nicole*
James I. Packer — *Gordon D. Fee*
R. C. Sproul — *Richard Lovelace*
Douglas Stuart — *J. Ramsey Michaels*

PREFACE BY
HAROLD J. OCKENGA

BAKER BOOK HOUSE
Grand Rapids, Michigan

ISBN: 0-8010-6733-2
Printed in the United States of America

To **Harold John Ockenga**
a stalwart upholder of biblical authority and inerrancy
throughout his years of ministry
1930–1980
and his presidency of
Gordon-Conwell Theological Seminary
1969–1979
we respectfully and gratefully dedicate this book

Preface

The modern controversy among evangelicals over the inspiration of Scripture is the reason for this book *Inerrancy and Common Sense.* The seeds of this struggle have been lying dormant in the environment of theological seminaries, denominations, Bible conferences, churches, colleges, and related institutions for several decades. Suddenly they seem to have sprouted and are growing apace. Organizations and individuals alike are being pressed with questions. People who work together to evangelize, to educate youth, and to operate the machinery of our denominations are aware of the theological implications of these questions. They need to express their convictions.

Two views confront each other: one, that Scripture is inerrant in all that it teaches—what Scripture teaches, God teaches; the other, that Scripture is inerrant in matters of faith and practice only—what is taught in other realms may be mistaken. The Gordon-Conwell Basis of Faith states: "The sixty-six canonical books of the Bible, as originally written, were inspired of God, hence free from error.

They constitute the only infallible guide in life and practice." Our faculty and trustees subscribe to this statement.

Some members of the faculty desired to express themselves jointly on the subject and now submit the enclosed essays to the Christian public. These essays all affirm an inerrant Bible, accepted under the rules of common-sense interpretation. With such elasticity, there should be little controversy about its authority. As president of the institution I take pleasure in commending this book, although such a commendation does not necessarily imply agreement with every detail in every paper.

Harold John Ockenga
Gordon-Conwell Theological Seminary

Contents

Introduction

The title of this volume may suggest to many minds two incompatible notions. Some readers may think that in dealing with difficulties and apparent contradictions anyone who maintains the doctrine of the inerrancy of Scripture is bound to propose explanations which are so contrived that he must of necessity have abandoned common sense in order to believe in them. If one desires to keep a firm hold on common sense and a sane approach to the Scriptures, they feel, one will have to leave behind the doctrine of inerrancy! But the authors of the present volume are hoping to combine these two features: a firm belief in the plenary inspiration and inerrancy of Holy Writ on the one hand, and a robust adherence to common sense on the other. They all share the conviction that a high view of Scripture is fully compatible with the sound pursuit of scholarship, and that the confession that the Bible is free from error is not necessarily a confining or restricting one.

The essays of this volume are all written by people who are members of the faculty of Gordon-Conwell Theological Seminary, either full-time, or in limited but regular involvement. Although the book is to be seen more as a sampling than as a full exposition of the view (or views) about Scripture represented at this seminary, it should give the reader some idea of the faculty's understanding of and commitment to its statement that the Bible is "inspired of God, hence free from error."

If there is one lesson that can be learned from this symposium, it is that a person's commitment to biblical inerrancy says little about the basis on which that person has accepted Scripture as the Word of God, and by no means necessarily predetermines the way in which that person interprets Scripture. These two matters—the epistemological question and the hermeneutical question—are at least as important as inerrancy itself. All the essays in this book are concerned to some degree with one or the other of these questions, or with both; and the discussion of them yields no consensus. The present volume therefore makes no claim of presenting anything like a full-orbed doctrine of Scripture. Rather it grows out of the responses of professors to questions raised by students on a particular occasion.

A symposium on the inerrancy of Scripture was held at Gordon-Conwell in May 1975, chaired by Roger Nicole. Eric Lemmon, Ramsey Michaels, James Packer, and Douglas Stuart made initial presentations which were followed by a panel discussion and questions from the floor. Professor Lemmon then took the initiative to make plans for the gathering of the papers to be included in this book. A tribute must be rendered to his diligence in securing them and in making comments that were helpful in preparing them for publication. When he decided not to continue with the project, the undersigned assumed jointly the duties of editorship. We would like also to record our gratitude to Holly Greening and Corinne Languedoc, who typed the essays; to Paul Mirecki, who annotated them with a view to securing uniformity in matters such as capitalization, footnote references, and so forth; and to Ray Wiersma, of the Baker Book House, and his associates for their diligent labors and unfailing courtesy.

A word remains to be said about the nature of the eight essays and the order in which they appear. We begin with Richard Lovelace's paper as providing a historical vista as well as supplying some suggestions for an evangelical strategy with reference to inerrancy. The essays of the two editors relate to dogmatics, Michaels making a comparison between the terminology of verbal inspiration and that of inerrancy, and Nicole seeking to provide a definition of inerrancy that fits with the phenomena of Scripture. Douglas Stuart directs his attention to the textual transmission of Scripture, with illustrations drawn from Old Testament textual criticism.

The last four essays relate in a variety of ways to the difficult subject of the interpretation of Scripture. R. C. Sproul has analyzed the components involved in the hermeneutical principle of the Analogy of Faith. John Jefferson Davis deals with the interpretation of Genesis, and Gordon Fee with that of the Pauline Epistles, both of them with a view to establishing certain principles of more general application than the texts they directly study. Finally, James Packer relates the whole issue of inerrancy, inspiration, and interpretation to the practical ministry of preaching. Thus Old Testament studies, New Testament studies, church history, dogmatics, and practical theology are all given at least some representation in this symposium.

It is our hope that in spite of their limitations these contributions will be helpful and will represent a sane and balanced voice in the midst of a controversy which is sometimes characterized by more heat than light.

J. Ramsey Michaels
Roger Nicole
Gordon-Conwell Theological Seminary

RICHARD LOVELACE

1

Inerrancy: Some Historical Perspectives

American Christianity is flourishing, and at the center of this growth is the evangelical movement. This is not simply the judgment of evangelical optimists. The secular news media responded to the presidential campaign of 1976, which offered a choice between two professed evangelicals, by christening the bicentennial anniversary of America's founding "the Year of the Evangelical."[1] Sociologist Peter Berger has speculated that the country may be in the birthpangs of a religious "great awakening," and he is joined in this opinion by Andrew Greeley and George Gallup.[2] Respect for evangelical leadership has increased among scholars and administrators in the mainline denominations. Seminaries which have been outside the

1. Cf. "1976: 'The Year of the Evangelical,'" *Christian Century* 93 (Dec. 29, 1976), pp. 1165–66; David Kucharsky, "The Year of the Evangelical," *Christianity Today* 21 (Oct. 22, 1976), pp. 12–13.
2. *New York Times,* 19 June 1977, p. 32.

evangelical subculture for most of the twentieth century have been challenged by a large influx of new converts from the campus ministry, and many have been visibly moved in a conservative direction. At the 1977 meeting of the United Presbyterian Council of Theological Seminaries, non-Presbyterian Fuller Seminary was cited as a model on the growing edge of theological education because of its pioneering in the areas of mission and church growth.

It is ironic, if not surprising, that just at this juncture evangelicalism shows signs of being on the verge of internal collapse.[3] Many younger evangelicals have little *esprit de corps.* Some even want to abandon the name because its capacity for dividing Christians seems greater than its theological and historical value, and others because it is associated in their memories with too much pain and weakness. Blacks and evangelicals concerned for social demonstration of the gospel have squared off against an older generation who actively oppose their concerns or treat them with benign neglect; charismatics and non-charismatics are uneasy with one another; confessional orthodoxies and "relational theology" are keenly critical of one another's weaknesses. The most serious of these lines of division may be the enlarging chasm between some "establishment evangelicals" holding to a doctrine of Scripture which defines inerrancy in terms which insist upon entire accuracy in scientific and historical matters, and those who have developed a doctrine of limited inerrancy which confines biblical infallibility to matters of faith and practice. A 1961 survey among American clergy reported in *Christianity Today* that 12 percent classify themselves as liberals, 14 percent as neoorthodox, and 74 percent as evangelicals. The last group is broken down into 35 percent Fundamentalists (who hold to total inerrancy) and 39 percent Conservatives (who hold to less than total iner-

---

3. Cf. Carl F. H. Henry, *Evangelicals in Search of Identity* (Waco, TX: Word Books, 1976).

rancy).[4] These figures indicate both the extent to which evangelicalism has been recapturing the center of the American church, and the imminent threat of its own dissolution—through the weakening of its message, according to one perspective, or through a destructive schism which would reduce its strength by more than half, according to another.

The movement away from strict inerrancy in evangelicalism is not a new phenomenon. It has been under observation for a long time—at least since the publication of Edward J. Carnell's *Case for Orthodox Theology* in 1959, which elaborated on a suggestion very tentatively advanced by E. F. Harrison in 1958, that the Bible may contain errors derived from sources used by the biblical writers and incorporated by them without correction. In the 1960s more developed doctrines of limited inerrancy were openly advocated by Dewey M. Beegle and Daniel P. Fuller.[5] Through the middle 1970s the tone of critical observers in the mainstream of evangelicalism remained one of concerned but restrained scholarly argument. At the Lausanne Conference in 1974, however, Francis Schaeffer sounded a note of urgent warning concerning the spread of this doctrine in evangelical ranks; and in 1976 Harold Lindsell's *Battle for the Bible* precipitated a major crisis by naming individuals and institutions now associated with a looser doctrine of Scripture. Schaeffer insisted, "There is no use of evangelicalism seeming to get larger and larger, if at the same time appreciable parts . . . are getting soft at

---

4. Cited in Eui Whan Kim, "The Authority and Uniqueness of the Bible," in *Let the Earth Hear His Voice,* ed. J. D. Douglas (Minneapolis: World Wide Publications, 1975), p. 989. This refers to a survey published in *Christianity Today* 6 (Nov. 10, 1961), p. 115.

5. See E. J. Carnell, *The Case for Orthodoxy* (Philadelphia: Westminster Press, 1951), pp. 102–10; E. F. Harrison, "The Phenomena of Scripture," in *Revelation and the Bible,* ed. Carl F. H. Henry (Philadelphia: Presbyterian and Reformed, 1958), p. 249; Dewey M. Beegle, *The Inspiration of Scripture* (Philadelphia: Westminster Press, 1963); Daniel P. Fuller, "Warfield's View of Faith and History," *Journal of the Evangelical Theological Society* 11 (1968), pp. 80–81.

that which is the central core, namely the Scriptures.... We must... say most lovingly but clearly: evangelicalism is not consistently evangelical unless there is a line drawn between those who take a full view of Scripture and those who do not."[6] In a subsequent pamphlet Schaeffer observes that "holding to a strong view of Scripture or not holding to it is the watershed of the evangelical world."[7]

Lindsell faces the latent question in Schaeffer's challenge and articulates it with great clarity: "Is the term 'evangelical' broad enough in its meaning to include within it believers in inerrancy and believers in an inerrancy limited to matters of faith and practice?... It seems to me that those who believe in inerrancy are left with little choice except to stand for a definition of 'evangelical' that includes in it the notion of biblical inerrancy. This is especially true if inerrancy is really a watershed that determines where one ends up."[8] Lindsell comments that "numbers of our evangelical schools that at one time were on a platform now are on a slope. And a slope soon becomes a slide, and it does not take long for people and institutions to hit the bottom."[9] In a series of historical vignettes, Lindsell attempts to prove that the adoption of limited inerrancy in any sector of the church always leads in the process of history to the eventual destruction of the doctrinal core of Christianity in that sector.[10] He comments that what is beginning now is the third in a series of struggles over the authority of Scripture in the course of American Christianity, the first two being the Briggs-Warfield controversy in the 1890s and the Fundamentalist

6. Francis Schaeffer, "Form and Freedom in the Church," in *Let the Earth Hear His Voice*, pp. 364–65.

7. Francis Schaeffer, *No Final Conflict* (Downers Grove, IL: Inter-Varsity Press, 1975).

8. Harold Lindsell, *The Battle for the Bible* (Grand Rapids: Zondervan, 1976), p. 139.

9. Ibid., p. 134.

10. Ibid., ch. 8.

controversy of the 1920s and 30s. Lindsell concludes that "evangelical Christianity is engaged in the greatest battle of its history."[11] The force of these warnings has not diminished in the evangelical community; Lindsell's book has become a best seller, and Schaeffer has continued to press the same issues.

The effort to precipitate a decisive moment of crisis among evangelicals over the Scripture issue has, however, drawn rather mixed reviews. Carl Henry, the elder statesman of the evangelical movement, has endorsed Lindsell's concern over the inerrancy issue but worries about the risk of causing a crippling division in evangelical ranks.[12] A majority of observers have commented on both the danger of destroying what God has built through the years, and the poor strategy of starting fights among team members just as the game is being won. Others, like Donald Dayton, have more aggressively suggested that what Lindsell and Schaeffer are setting up as the historic Christian position on Scripture is not in reality the position of the Reformers but only part of the hardened structure of post-Reformation scholastic orthodoxy, imported into American Fundamentalism through the Princeton theologians A. A. Hodge and B. B. Warfield.[13] This is essentially the same contention which was raised against Hodge and Warfield by Charles Augustus Briggs and Henry Preserved Smith, in the first of the three controversies mentioned by Lindsell, and which has been reiterated since then by neoorthodox critics of evangelical orthodoxy.

In the body of this essay I want to address three issues raised by the current dispute over inerrancy, speaking as a historical theologian specializing in the history of evangeli-

11. Ibid., pp. 141, 200.

12. Carl F. H. Henry, Review of *The Battle for the Bible* in *New Review of Books and Religion* 1 (Sept. 1976), p. 7.

13. Donald Dayton, "Wrong Front: A Review of *The Battle for the Bible,*" in *The Other Side,* May/June 1976, pp. 36–39.

calism and the course of evangelical awakenings in the church:

1. Is Dayton's contention correct, or was the position represented by Lindsell and Schaeffer the normative position of the church on Scripture until the present century?

2. Is Lindsell correct in holding that church history demonstrates the rapid and inevitable decay of all varieties of limited inerrancy into subevangelical theologies?

3. Given the massive division among evangelicals on this issue, what is the most constructive strategy of healing to be followed in the future?

Was Total Inerrancy the Normative Position of the Church?

With the single exception of Theodore of Mopsuestia, the early church fathers (Barnabas, Clement of Rome, Justin Martyr, Athenagoras, Tertullian, Clement of Alexandria, Origen, Cyprian) treated Scripture as divinely inspired and absolutely authoritative, the very words of God. Quotations from Irenaeus may be advanced in support of plenary verbal inspiration.[14] All of this, however, could also be affirmed by most evangelical proponents of limited inerrancy, a fact which opposing critics often overlook. But Augustine is more explicit:

> I have learned to yield such respect and honour only to the canonical books of Scripture; of these do I most firmly believe that the authors were completely free from error. And if in these writings I am perplexed by anything which appears to me opposed to truth, I do not hesitate to suppose that either the *manuscript is faulty,* or the translator has not caught the meaning of what was said, or I myself have failed to understand it.[15]

---

14. Cf. J. Barton Payne, "The Biblical Interpretation of Irenaeus," in *Inspiration and Interpretation,* ed. John F. Walvoord (Grand Rapids: Wm. B. Eerdmans, 1957), pp. 11-66.

15. Augustine, Letter 82.3.

Eugene TeSelle's recent and definitive study of Augustine's theology states:

> He has confidence that whatever has been discovered about the world on the basis of reliable evidence cannot be inconsistent with the Bible, and, on the other hand, that where secular writers *are* clearly inconsistent with the Bible they can be proved, or at least believed, to be wrong, for Christ possesses (in the words of Colossians 2,3) "all the treasures of both wisdom and knowledge," *sapientia* and *scientia* (*De Gen. ad litt.*, I, 21, 41).[16]

On Augustine's letter J. K. S. Reid comments, "In other words, it is to the original documents and texts that inerrancy belongs; any apparent error must then be due to adventitious causes only."[17] The Hodge-Warfield position is therefore not merely an echo of Protestant orthodoxy; its germinal core is clearly stated by the foundational theologian of the Christian church.

Oswald Loretz, a Catholic theologian concerned to shift the church's position on Scripture away from factual inerrancy, concurs with Hermann Sasse's judgment that Augustine taught "that the Bible is free from mistakes, errors and contradictions even in its smallest details."[18] Loretz concludes that Augustine's position remained normative in the Roman Catholic Church until the Second Vatican Council. Thus the medieval church in the West continued to hold to total inerrancy until the eve of the Reformation.[19]

The position of the Reformers with respect to inspiration and inerrancy has been an area of extreme controversy among historians and theologians in the twentieth

---

16. Eugene TeSelle, *Augustine the Theologian* (New York: Herder and Herder, 1970), p. 206.
17. J. K. S. Reid, *The Authority of Scripture* (New York: Harper, 1957), p. 154.
18. Oswald Loretz, *The Truth of the Bible* (New York: Herder and Herder, 1968), p. 5.
19. Cf. *New Catholic Encyclopedia*, pp. 384–85, 513–18.

century. Most of this conflict seems to issue from the understandable tendency of neoorthodox theologians to read their reconstruction of Protestant doctrine back into the Reformers themselves, a tendency most evangelical scholars readily detect. As Clark Pinnock remarks, "It is as though between the medieval period and the age of Protestant orthodoxy there were a brief neoorthodox paradise in which such views were for a moment grasped, only to be quickly lost again, and rediscovered by Barth!"[20] It cannot be denied that the sixteenth-century Reformers had a spiritual power not always present in their scholastic successors, and it is also true that the evidence on this issue is complex, in both the cases of Luther and Calvin. Nevertheless, it seems clear that the magisterial Reformers remained consistently Augustinian in their approach to Scripture, as we might expect from their rootage in the Augustinian tradition.

Luther's reservations about the canonicity of some parts of Scripture are well known. It seems apparent, however, that with respect to the great bulk of the Bible that he did consider canonical, his approach does not differ from Augustine's. Witness some of Luther's statements on this issue. "St. Augustine, in a letter to St. Jerome, has put down a fine axiom—that only Holy Scripture is to be considered inerrant."[21] "It is impossible that Scripture should contradict itself; it only appears so to senseless and obstinate hypocrites."[22] On Jonah and the whale: "Who would believe it and not consider it a lie and a fable if it did not stand recorded in Scripture?"[23] "We ascribe the entire

20. Clark H. Pinnock, *Biblical Revelation—The Foundation of Christian Theology* (Chicago: Moody Press, 1971), p. 153.

21. Martin Luther, *Werke,* Weimer edition (WA), vol. 34, I, p. 347. Cited by John W. Montgomery, "Lessons from Luther on the Inerrancy of Holy Writ," in *God's Inerrant Word,* ed. John W. Montgomery (Minneapolis: Bethany Fellowship, 1974), pp. 66–68, from which the following citations are also drawn.

22. Ibid., vol. 9, p. 356.

23. Ibid., vol. 19, p. 219.

Holy Scripture to the Holy Spirit."[24] "Not only the words which the Holy Spirit and Scripture use are divine, but also the phrasing."[25] "The Holy Spirit is not a fool or a drunkard to express one point, not to say one word, in vain."[26] Luther's grappling with apparent historical discrepancies in Scripture did not move him away from Augustine's position: "Thus he seeks to squelch what he calls 'the foolhardy geniuses who immediately shout that an obvious error has been committed' by averring that finally 'it is the Holy Spirit alone who knows and understands all things.' ... To imply that it contained error was to him not only contrary to what the Scripture itself testified concerning its truthfulness and inerrancy, but, above all, an insolent affront to God who gave it."[27]

In the case of Calvin, recent scholarship seems to be reversing the earlier conclusions of Emile Doumergue and others who argued that the Reformer was not committed to entire inerrancy. In his 1952 monograph Edward Dowey, Jr., not a warm friend of this doctrine, insisted that Calvin's approach to Scripture was essentially that of Hodge and Warfield:

> It is always to the text before him, never to the original text of Scripture, that Calvin attributes such errors as his exegesis discovers.... Doumergue, Clavier, and others are wrong to introduce Calvin's free *a posteriori* exegetical method as evidence against his holding a dictation theory concerning the origin of Scripture....
>
> The openness of Calvin's exegesis, by which he leaves points undecided, which is so highly prized as evidence by those who think Calvin no verbal inspirationist, actually is evidence to the contrary. The obscurities in the text are allowed for theologically.... They are designed by the

24. Ibid., vol. 54, p. 35.
25. Ibid., vol. 40, III, p. 254.
26. Ibid., vol. 54, p. 39.
27. Eugene F. A. Klug, *From Luther to Chemnitz: On Scripture and the Word* (Kampen: J. H. Kok, 1971), pp. 109–10.

> Spirit to promote humility. But neither these obscurities nor obvious mistakes are ever explained in a way that would imply any admixture of human fallibility in Scripture, as if the inspired writer were not a perfect instrument of transmission for the message he received. . . .
>
> To Calvin the theologian an error in Scripture is unthinkable. Hence the endless harmonizing, the explaining and interpreting of passages that seem to contradict or to be inaccurate. But Calvin the critical scholar recognizes mistakes with a disarming ingenuousness. The mistake or the gloss is simply a blunder made by an ignorant copyist.[28]

James I. Packer comments that the small number of passages in Calvin's exegesis which seem to imply error in the text fall into four categories: accommodation to common forms of speech or the human phenomenal perspective, as in the treatment of astronomical data; textual alterations; loose and paraphrastic quotations of the Old Testament by apostolic writers; and cases where the text does not intend to assert error, as in the topical rather than chronological handling of events in the Synoptic Gospels.[29] Modern evangelical proponents of total inerrancy handle such instances in the same way.

During the seventeenth and eighteenth centuries, Lutheran and Reformed orthodoxy continued to hold the unlimited inerrancy of Scripture, often going beyond the Reformers to assert that the biblical authors were wholly passive, and that the Bible was literally dictated by the Holy Spirit in the process of inspiration.[30] The evangelical

---

28. Edward A. Dowey, Jr., *The Knowledge of God in Calvin's Theology* (New York: Columbia University Press, 1952), pp. 103–04.

29. James I. Packer, "Calvin's View of Scripture," in *God's Inerrant Word,* ed. John Warwick Montgomery (Minneapolis: Bethany Fellowship, 1974), pp. 105–07.

30. Jack Bartlett Rogers, following the argument of C. A. Briggs and many later commentators, concludes that it is anachronistic to read the Hodge-Warfield position on inerrancy back into the authors of the Westminster Confession (*Scripture in the Westminster Confession* [Kampen: J. H. Kok, 1966]). Certainly what the Confession contains is (taken by itself) a classic statement of inerrancy in

leaders of the Great Awakening did not depart from Augustine's position. John Wesley expressed a very radical trust in Scripture: "If there be any mistakes in the Bible, there may well be a thousand. If there be one falsehood in that book, it did not come from the God of truth."[31] While I am not aware of any text in which Jonathan Edwards explicitly affirms total inerrancy, his handling of Scripture seems to reflect this degree of confidence; and it is significant that the third of his five signs of the operation of the Holy Spirit in genuine renewal of the church is a heightened respect for the authority of Scripture.[32]

It seems clear that the Augustinian position of entire confidence in biblical inerrancy was normative in the various streams of Christian orthodoxy at least until the Darwinian revolution cast doubt upon biblical cosmology and anthropology. The position of Hodge and Warfield is not, as Briggs maintained, a new departure which diverges from a previous main tradition of limited inerrancy, but is simply a restatement of the classical position. The question may be raised—and certainly should be raised—whether the Augustinian doctrine of Scripture is adequate and defensible after Darwin, but limited inerrancy ought not to be read back into earlier theologians in order to give it credibility today. As Warfield points out, the doctrine of limited inerrancy originated among Socinians after the Reformation, and was transmitted in the seventeenth and eighteenth centuries by "Arminians" whose theological

---

matters of faith and practice; but it seems that Rogers does not effectively meet the force of B. B. Warfield's arguments in *The Westminster Assembly and Its Work* (New York: Oxford University Press, 1931) and *Limited Inspiration* (Philadelphia: Presbyterian and Reformed, 1974), especially his contention that Briggs's argument forces the Westminster divines out of harmony with their contemporaries on the Continent.

31. John Wesley, *Journal,* Wednesday, July 24, 1776.

32. Jonathan Edwards, "Distinguishing Marks of a Work of the Spirit of God," in *The Great Awakening,* ed. C. C. Goen (New Haven: Yale University Press, 1972), pp. 226–88.

stance was considerably removed from the orthodoxy of James Arminius and John Wesley.[33]

Is Limited Inerrancy a Slope Which Leads Inevitably to Heresy?

At first glance, Lindsell's postulate of the inevitable decline of sectors of the church which espouse limited inerrancy seems to be an example of the logical fallacy of *post hoc, propter hoc* (after a thing, and therefore because of it). Using this logic, we might question the integrity of the theological positions not only of the Reformers, but also of Paul and Jesus, since the traditions flowing from all of them have suffered uncomfortably long periods of decline.

Theological decline is after all a much more complex matter than the simple outworking of flawed conceptual positions. Its most important dimensions are probably personal and spiritual. A careful study of the origins of heterodoxy indicates that heresy develops best in two theological environments. It can readily originate in a theologically invertebrate, existential pietism, whose incipient weaknesses are worked out fully by a second generation. But it can just as easily arise in a dead, rationalistic conceptual orthodoxy, through the mutation of the second generation's reacting against the perceived weaknesses of the elders. No student of early twentieth-century American Fundamentalism who is acquainted with the classical evangelicalism of Spener, Francke, Edwards, and Wesley can fail to be impressed with the comparative theological and spiritual weakness of the later period. The shift of the center of gravity in the American church from evangelical to liberal and neoorthodox leadership is a very compli-

33. Warfield, *Westminster Assembly*, p. 203; cf. Robert Preus, *The Inspiration of Scripture* (London: Oliver and Boyd Ltd., 1955), pp. 81–85.

cated historical process, but it seems to have involved a theological mutation in the children of evangelical leaders, reacting against and losing confidence in their elders, while involved in an educational process which exerted terrific pressure on their minds through the power of organized systems of non-Christian thought. Francis Schaeffer traces the decline of modern Western culture to the spiritual decline in the church, which in turn is due to the rejection of propositional revelation and the inerrancy of Scripture by church leaders.[34] Behind that rejection, however, is often a crisis of confidence in the intellectual, theological, and spiritual integrity of the evangelical movement within the church. In the case of early twentieth-century Fundamentalism, this may have been understandable. As Pogo remarks, "We have met the enemy, and he is us."

We may also question whether the rejection of total biblical inerrancy is the most important controlling doctrinal factor behind theological decay. Lindsell cites American Unitarianism as an instance in which doctrinal decline has followed from a rejection of biblical authority.[35] Actually this example proves something very different. Early American Unitarianism through William Ellery Channing was quite orthodox in its doctrine of Scripture, if not in its total system derived from the Bible. Usually it presented itself as a biblicist reaction against the metaphysical theory of Nicaea and Chalcedon. The first major departure from conservative Unitarianism was Ralph Waldo Emerson, who inaugurated the tradition which prevails in the denomination today. In 1838 he found himself unable to continue to administer the Lord's Supper, because the celebration of redemption in Christ was meaningless to him. It is significant that Andrews Norton, a leading Unitarian theologian after Channing, called for (and got) the sup-

---

34. E.g., *Death in the City* (Chicago: Inter-Varsity Press, 1969).
35. Lindsell, *Battle for the Bible,* pp. 143–44.

port of Charles Hodge in attacking the new Unitarian left wing through a common appeal to inerrant Scripture.[36] Apparently the root of Unitarian decline was not a deficiency in its doctrine of biblical authority, but the failure to hear the Holy Spirit speaking through the Word, and therefore a decay in its perception of the transcendent holiness of God, the depth of human sin, and the glory of Christ's redemptive work. Ironically enough, on the other hand, Charles Hodge, although a staunch upholder of the doctrine of biblical inerrancy, could argue loosely that even if there are what appear to be factual errors in Scripture, they are as insignificant as specks on the Parthenon.[37] The casual concession in Hodge's illustration did not lead to the inevitable decline which Lindsell's theorem would cause us to expect; it led instead to the more carefully defined doctrine of A. A. Hodge and Warfield! We learn from these examples that a deficient doctrine of Scripture is not always the primary cause of doctrinal decay, and that a less than perfect view of Scripture does not *inevitably* lead to such decay.

It could even be argued that an excessive *tightening* of the doctrine of Scripture resulted in the loss of the children of evangelicals in the early decades of this century. Theology is like some kinds of machinery; if one fails to allow sufficient play in certain areas, and turns the bolts too far, parts break off under the stress of life. Perhaps the

36. William Hutchinson, *The Transcendentalist Ministers* (Boston: Beacon Press, 1965), p. 86n.

37. We refer particularly to the passage in Hodge's *Systematic Theology* (New York: Charles Scribner's Sons, 1871) in which he states: "The errors in matters of fact which skeptics search out bear no proportion to the whole. No sane man would deny that the Parthenon was built of marble, even if here and there a speck of sandstone should be detected in its structure" (vol. I, p. 170). This illustration, which was meant to emphasize the trivial character of alleged errors, has at times been interpreted as implying that Hodge held that the original text of Scripture included minor flaws. But this conclusion is inconsistent with Hodge's clear effort (in the immediate context of this statement and elsewhere) to resolve apparent errors and defend the integrity of the original text.

Lausanne Covenant's formula concerning Scripture, which holds that it is "without error in all that it affirms," maintains a balance of play and sufficient tightness to do justice to the subtle process by which the Holy Spirit limits the boundaries of our thought as He speaks through the Word. Possibly the Fundamentalists would not have lost so many of their children to liberalism if they had been armed with such a formula.[38] But we must also take into account not only the fact that men like Briggs and Smith were operating with an inadequate doctrine of Scripture, but that they had surrendered many crucial areas of evangelical faith which current evangelical proponents of limited inerrancy are holding fast. The rate of slippage may be much reduced in our current situation, in which so many nonevangelical sectors of the church seem to be moving back toward a stronger doctrine of Scripture.

Orthodoxy on the single point of Scripture has never been a reliable indication of spiritual vigor or value to the kingdom of God. The worst enemies of the evangelical renewal under Spener and Francke were the leaders of the Lutheran state church, who shared their commitment to confessional orthodoxy. The whole development of Puritan theology culminating in the work of Edwards was designed to attack and correct a merely "notional" propositional orthodoxy, which Puritans considered the worst enemy of true Christianity, and which still remains a standing scandal in some parts of the church today. Systematic

---

38. *Let the Earth Hear His Voice,* p. 3. It has been suggested that those who favor limited inerrancy shift to this formula in order to affirm that Scripture speaks with strict factual accuracy in the overwhelming number of instances in which it deals with history or cosmology, but contains minor errors in matters which it does not intend to affirm. It is objected that this formula commits what literary critics call the intentional fallacy, and that we do not have access to the author's intent; but the analogy with literary criticism breaks down in view of the illuminating ministry of the Holy Spirit, and Lausanne's formula may indeed be the one which most carefully preserves the delicate balance of art and spiritual dependence which results in sound hermeneutical practice.

orthodoxy which does not apprehend the balance of the Word and Spirit held by the Puritans and Reformers has proved to be an easy target when confronted by neoorthodoxy's emphasis on existential faith-encounter through the work of the Holy Spirit, which is a deficient but recognizable copy of the classic evangelical balance.

Thus the rigor of any individual's *doctrine* of Scripture tells us little about his or her spiritual depth and theological fruitfulness. Some with a higher doctrine of Scripture seem largely deaf to the renewing voice of the Spirit through the Word, and express this failure in their lives; some with a lower doctrine are powerful and productive agents in God's kingdom. We need only think of theologians like P. T. Forsyth and Helmut Thielicke to recognize that a theologian's *position* is not everything; his or her spiritual *direction* is also important. Those who are dynamically impelled by God's Word to cross over from liberal theology toward orthodoxy breathe out life in their teaching; those whose hearts are averted from God while their heads are clinging to orthodoxy breathe out death, and in reality are crossing the bridge in the other direction. As the Preacher says, "A living dog is better than a dead lion" (Eccles. 9:4).

The example of Karl Barth proves that a gravely deficient doctrine of Scripture does not invalidate an individual's ability to apprehend biblical orthodoxy at many points. As Klaas Runia indicates, Barth's view of Scripture is considerably below that of limited inerrancy, since it admits that the Bible's capacity for error "also extends to its religious or theological content."[39] Despite the weaknesses of Barth's reconstruction of Reformation thought, however, and the divorce from history which his view of revelation risks, it is rare to find him resisting and rejecting apostolic teaching, and he has constantly been attacked by liberals as

39. Klaas Runia, *Karl Barth's Doctrine of Holy Scripture* (Grand Rapids: Wm. B. Eerdmans, 1962), p. 60.

a crypto-Fundamentalist.[40] This leads us to suspect that in some neoorthodox figures the actual heart-commitment to Scripture is much stronger than their theoretical definition of it, which is employed in combination with existential metaphysics to drown out liberal critics, as the squid confuses its pursuers with a cloud of ink. Bad *views* of Scripture are so often counterbalanced by a right *use* of Scripture that honest believers must have some reservations about Lindsell's theorem.

But while Barth's theology did not entirely destroy itself because of an erroneous doctrine of Scripture, *Barthians* are another matter. It is common knowledge that apprentices trained in his approach have been collapsing regularly during the last several decades, some of them moving even outside the orbit of theism. Here is William Hamilton describing the decay in his apprehension of Scripture:

> Is the theologian reading the Bible? The Bible is a strange book that does not come alive to him as it is supposed to. There are still some pieces of it that come alive, to be sure, although he is not sure why or how: this psalmist, that prophetic call, a piece or two of Job, perhaps even some words of Jesus.
>
> The theologian is alienated from the Bible, just as he is alienated from God and the church. This alienation may not last. If it doesn't last, fine; if it does last, the theologian will have some piercing questions to ask of himself. But there are wrong ways (Karl Barth) and right ways to overcome this alienation, and for now he has to be honest with himself, with the God before whom he stands in unbelief and he must wait.[41]

Barth's doctrine does not treat the Bible as a Parthenon with specks; it describes it rather as a dark night sky il-

40. Ibid., pp. 61–62.

41. William Hamilton, "Thursday's Child," in *Radical Theology and the Death of God*, ed. Thomas J. J. Altizer and William Hamilton (Indianapolis: Bobbs-Merrill, 1966), pp. 89–90.

luminated with occasional stars of insight. Such a view of truth is very subject to occasional atmospheric disturbances which obscure the view, and offers little incentive to keep searching until they blow over.

Most evangelical proponents of limited inerrancy hold a version which is closer to Hodge's Parthenon metaphor, and therefore more secure from immediate collapse than Barth's position. Nevertheless even small allowances for error or ignorance in scientific and historical matters can have immediate and unforeseen effects in blocking our perception of biblical truth. A case in point is the comment I recently heard from an evangelical seminary teacher, who remarked that since Paul was wrong about women he was probably wrong about homosexuality also, and urged that practicing homosexuals be admitted to the church and ordained. Paul Jewett, whose book on the biblical approach to sexuality probably occasioned this remark, would undoubtedly argue that this comment is incorrect both as a representation of his position and as a deduction from it.[42] Nevertheless this is an instance where the adoption of limited inerrancy has brought about an instantaneous loss of traction in a critical area of Christian ethics. It is extremely difficult to isolate matters of faith and practice from issues related to science and history. Dewey Beegle's comment that human reason can make such judgments relatively easily reveals an amazing lack of awareness of the history of rationalism, and the rapid erosion of faith which always occurs when this principle is introduced.[43] Barth's appeal to the Holy Spirit for the sorting out of grain and chaff in Scripture is a much more sophisticated approach, but ultimately introduces a subjectivism which destroys the balance between the Spirit and the Word. Clark Pinnock

---

42. Paul Jewett, *Man as Male and Female* (Grand Rapids: Wm. B. Eerdmans, 1975).

43. Dewey M. Beegle, *Scripture, Tradition, and Infallibility* (Grand Rapids: Wm. B. Eerdmans, 1973), pp. 62–64.

may well be right when he says that a doctrine of complete inerrancy is vital "because the *sola scriptura* principle cannot be maintained without it."[44]

The fundamental rationale behind the doctrine of total inerrancy is the connection between the Christian faith and history. Scientific details in the realm of cosmology have little immediate effect on faith but the notion of incorrect history in Scripture has devastating implications for essential biblical doctrines. For most of this century theologians have been trying to rig a tandem harness between what C. S. Lewis calls the "great myth" of human evolution and the doctrines of creation, the fall, and redemption; the results have usually eviscerated essential features of Pauline teaching.[45] The road between limited inerrancy and a developed program of demythologizing Scripture may be very short. And beyond that the road to a totally unanchored existential gnosticism may be even shorter. Both neoorthodox theology and the proponents of limited inerrancy seek to secure the Christian faith in a position which is invulnerable to attack on scientific and historical grounds. In the eyes of the world, however, they may ultimately simply be retreating from defeat on the battlefields of reality to become rulers of a dream world of symbolism, which is what the world has always suspected Christians were offering. Warfield was uncannily accurate in predicting the effect of limited inerrancy on theological reality:

> Dr. Smith's impulse arises not out of faith, but out of despair. He cannot fight the battle of the book on the old lines. He must yield the husk that he may save the kernel. Possibly, if the country around be yielded to the ravages of the enemy, they may spare the citadel; or mayhap the citadel may be defended if the surrounding country be

---

44. Pinnock, *Biblical Revelation*, p. 74.

45. C. S. Lewis, *Christian Reflections*, ed. Walter Hooper (Grand Rapids: Wm. B. Eerdmans, 1967), pp. 82–93.

> given up; or perhaps, even, it may be removed to shadow-land, where earthly darts cannot reach it. We cannot hold the Bible in the face of modern assault. Let us hold to a shadowy Bible within the Bible, which is removed beyond the reach of scientific tests, and in which we may, therefore, manage to believe *malgré* science—if we any longer wish to believe in it.[46]

Now that Roman Catholics, in the wake of Vatican II, are largely retreating from the Augustianian position to one of limited inerrancy,[47] it may be the peculiar task of evangelical Christians to uphold the classical position in the late twentieth century. In the post-Darwinian era Western Christians have developed an inveterate habit of bowing to fallen human reason in the form of scientific authority, and yielding up whole departments of existence to the psychologists, biologists, anthropologists, and sociologists, rather than doing the hard intellectual labor of rethinking these disciplines biblically. We have taken apart the Bible at the world's direction, to discard the wheat and save the chaff, instead of winnowing the world's thinking by biblical norms. In so doing we may have ruined our apologetics and surrendered our culture to the rule of non-Christian thought. The Bible has been an embarrassment to theologians in this century; it has been sequestered in a back room of church life like a garrulous and senile relative at a family reunion. But in this it has only followed the pattern of Jesus Himself, the carpenter's son who embarrassed Israel by His lack of messianic splendor. Note, however, that His practice was to treat the Scripture as infallible in all respects, and His counsel to us is that those who annul the smallest fragment of biblical truth will be counted least in the kingdom (Matt. 5:19). He fulfilled and exemplified the word of Isaiah which stands also as an admonition to us: "To this one I will look, to him

46. Warfield, *Limited Inspiration,* p. 52.
47. Pinnock, *Biblical Revelation,* pp. 172–74.

who is humble and contrite of spirit, and who trembles at My word" (66:2, NASB).

But there is another perspective which even those committed to total inerrancy should keep in mind. It is epitomized in the account I once heard from a famous theologian of how his faith had been shattered by his first encounter with destructive biblical criticism, and would have been lost except for the assistance of Karl Barth's theology. This man was able to salvage his spiritual sanity at the expense of his theological consistency, with the aid of limited inerrancy. His experience undoubtedly typifies that of many others. I wonder if there are any among us today willing to risk the spiritual sanity of our children by riveting their faith to Wesley's iron axiom, *Falsus in uno, falsus in omnibus?* I would suggest that we should leave the option of a very high view of limited inerrancy as a secondary system for them to fall back upon if they are confronted with what seem to be irreconcilably conflicting data of Scripture and of ordinary factuality. This is not to surrender the case for unlimited inerrancy; it is simply to recognize the strength of systematic denials of the biblical world view in our culture and arm our troops accordingly. It may also be simple humility and not incipient unbelief to admit that total inerrancy *could* be claiming a dimension of truth for Scripture which Scripture indeed does not claim, and that the discernment of the mind of Christ in the written Word is a task which demands artistry beyond any formula we can devise, and which calls for utter dependence on the risen Word and His Spirit. As the Hodges, Warfield, and James Orr have admitted, God *could* have committed His truth to Scripture in the manner specified by Daniel Fuller, or even by Barth and Brunner. He did not *have* to adjust to human sin and ignorance by allowing the intrusion of minor errors into the transmission of major truths, but He *could* have done so. If we make a strong case for total inerrancy, our admission of these possibilities will not encourage others in unbelief. Rather, it will keep them in a basically evangelical doctrinal commitment and in dialogue with us, until their reservations can be resolved.

What Is the Most Constructive Strategy of Healing?

This suggests that there may be a rationale, and indeed a necessity, for advocates of total and limited inerrancy to continue to work together in mutual respect and love as well as reciprocal concern. Ultimately both of these positions are aiming at the same goal: to find a formula for biblical authority which will most effectively guarantee that future generations will approach the Scriptures in an attitude of dependent faith, so that they will hear the Holy Spirit speaking through the Word on every crucial issue, and so that it will in fact be "the only infallible rule of faith and practice." In reality both are aiming only to guarantee the retention of cardinal doctrinal and ethical teaching, although those who espouse total inerrancy maintain that this cannot be done without a more inclusive definition of truth and error.

An examination of Western church history in this century suggests that looser and stricter views of biblical authority have exercised a complementary function in the life of the church. Strict inerrancy has been needed so that at least a part of the church could remain theologically sane, and this has been nurtured in ghettoes of Christians who have not usually been in very close touch with the front edge of secular intellectual culture. Those in other parts of the church who have been immersed in that culture have experienced, first, a magnetic field of antibiblical thought of such overpowering intensity that it has almost inevitably distorted their faith to some degree; and second, a missionary task that has seemingly almost required the surrender, or at least the suppression, of the issue of biblical inerrancy. Those who work with the cultured despisers of religion have felt a strong compulsion to avoid putting before them any stumbling block except the cross, and have often chosen to focus their apologetics on the critical issues of sin and redemption rather than on the rationally prior issue of the source of intellectual authority. Sometimes their very lack of commitment to the biblical cosmology has qualified them to reach intellectual captives of modern culture whose minds would stumble at an inerrant Bible, but whose hearts respond to the core of the gospel.

Obviously both these types of Christians need one another. Those who face the roaring abyss of unbelief need the advocates of inerrancy to keep recalling them to theological sanity. Those who are fortunate enough to dwell close to the glowing reality of the biblical world, among traditions and fellow believers who reinforce their perception of that world rather than attenuating it, need contact with those whose post is on the frontiers of secular life, to remind them that the church's primary task is saving the world rather than maintaining antiseptic purity of thought for its own sake, and to allow them to exercise their vocation of healing the battered minds of those on the front line.

The segments of the church I have described above are not subcultures within evangelicalism. Rather, the first group is composed of evangelicals, and the second of many (perhaps most) nonevangelicals. Among Protestants an unusual number of the latter group often turn out to be ex-evangelicals repelled by the weakness of their parent culture or captured by the attractions of the liberal church which mediates between evangelicalism and the secular world. I would suggest that if this relationship of complementary need exists across the evangelical border, a lesser complementary polarity can be tolerated within evangelical ranks.

This recommendation may come as a shock to Christians in those removed enclaves where total inerrancy is uncontested. But the extent of the bloodletting which would be necessary to solve by surgical excision the problem of differing views on biblical authority would occasion an even greater shock. To cure the evangelical establishment by ruling out those currently holding limited inerrancy would require the expulsion of more than half of evangelicalism, and would split many institutions down the middle in the kind of trauma we have already seen modeled for us at Concordia Seminary. Surely it is not unreasonable to suggest that the risks of surgery are too high. It would take years for the evangelical consensus to recover, and in the meantime we would succeed only in snatching defeat from the jaws of victory. Those who contend that the present growth of evangelicalism is meaningless without uniform adherence to total inerrancy are radically misreading the situation, because they have magnified their legitimate concern for one jewel of truth which is in their custody until it eclipses their vision of the treasury of jewels which is being poured out across the church at large in the process of evangelical renewal. David Hubbard is right to defend the new Fuller Statement of Faith as a clear and beautiful exposition of essential evangelical truth, a declaration which is winning nonevangelical observers and institutions to the core of evangelical doctrine.[48] For those of us who are laboring side by side with Fuller graduates in rebuilding the fallen structures of faith in the mainline denominations, the suggestion that we should suddenly turn upon our colaborers and throw them from the wall smacks of Sanballat, not of Nehemiah.

Many proponents of total inerrancy will immediately respond to this approach with the word *compromise,* and will suggest that it was this kind of accommodation which sold the larger denominations into subevangelical captivity in the early decades of this century. If history proves anything, it proves the reverse of this. In the Briggs trial, the

48. *Theology, News and Notes* (published for the Fuller Theological Seminary alumni), Special Issue, 1976, p. 32.

Scopes trial, and many aspects of the Fundamentalist-Modernist controversy, evangelicals won the battle, but lost the war. Individual operations were successful, but the patient nearly died. Just as some young people within Missouri Synod Lutheranism are now drawn to Seminex out of sympathy, the ugly spectacle of Christians persecuting other Christians over what appeared to be doctrinal minutiae became part of the catalyst which caused a generation of Fundamentalists to move in a liberal direction. Another kind of surgical excision, the separation of those holding total inerrancy from the major denominations, enabled them to keep broadcasting a clear biblical signal. But if it were not for those who "compromised" and remained within the major denominations to labor for reformation, the numerical expansion of evangelicalism in this century would have been radically curtailed and the current movement of the larger denominations in a biblical direction would have been impossible. Those of us who are finding success, and the blessing of the Lord, in the endeavor to recapture the central fortress of American Christianity for the evangelical faith—which held it in the nineteenth century, and which lost it because of our weakness and the world's deceiving strength—are seeking to build a central coalition of evangelicals and recovered conservatives from other sectors in the church, so that the core of Christian doctrine summed up in the Fuller Statement can be not simply uttered in the darkness of a few evangelical ghettoes, but shouted from the housetops in broad daylight before the nations. It seems obvious folly to us to cease cooperation with evangelical brothers and sisters whose view appears to us weak with respect to inerrancy, at the same time that we are reaching fruitful accord with church leaders who are crawling out of the ruins of neoorthodoxy and trying to recover the central foundations of their faith.

This calls our attention to an important fact in the current struggle over inerrancy. Those who seem to be calling for expulsion, or at least for discipline, of evangelicals holding limited inerrancy, reflect a style of ecclesiology which is only one of two main options in the history of responsible churchmanship. The option they hold is usually attacked as Donatism or separatism, but this may not be entirely fair. It defines denominational expressions within the larger church as voluntary societies for the propagation of purified, extensive doctrinal systems, and it rationalizes its separation from other Christian groups by the thesis that involvement with them demands a degree of compromise which leads insensibly away from a clear and sharp perception of biblical truth.[49] The other ecclesiological option is that which seeks to establish denominational boundaries on the basis of maximal inclusion of Christians around a minimal core of Christian faith, according to the maxim of Rupert Meldenius: Unity in essentials, liberty in inessentials, charity in all things. The first option labors *mainly* to preserve the purity and clarity of the whole counsel of God; the second labors *mainly* to build a visible demonstration of the unity of the body of

49. This is clearly Schaeffer's perspective: "If we say that Christianity is truth yet for any reason, including evangelism, we blur the line between liberal theology and biblical Christianity in the area of religious cooperation, we lose credibility with the world today which does not believe that truth exists in any form" ("Form and Freedom," p. 361). This statement seems simply to deny the validity of a real calling from God to evangelicals working in the mainline denominations, yet such a calling is strongly attested by the blessing of God on burgeoning churches and the renewing spread of central evangelical doctrines among many ex-liberals and recovered ex-evangelicals. Speaking the truth in love to Dr. Schaeffer, we must say two things very urgently. First, "liberal theology" is too indefinite a phrase to describe all the forms of nonevangelical theology which abound today; some of these are antithetical to the gospel, and some are merely incomplete forms of evangelical faith. Second, many "liberals" are themselves ex-evangelicals, or simply Christians converted in their early youth, who have been theologically crippled by corrosive seminary education. The strengths in Schaeffer's position spring from his disengagement from church involvement which would occasion compromise, but there are also weaknesses in his understanding which flow from his lack of first-hand contact with a wide spectrum of "liberals" in person and on paper. We expect to see this weakness healed, even as we appeal to him for continued witness against our own weakness.

Christ. It may not be equivocation to maintain that these two ecclesiologies are both needed if the unity and biblical sanity of Christendom are to be achieved, and it may not be sentimentality to maintain that they both need one another.

Now it is significant in this context to ask which of these ecclesiological strategies has characterized evangelicalism in the past. The historical answer is quite clear. The first strategy, which seeks for purity at the risk of separation, has its roots in the Reformation but then develops in diverse streams of *confessional orthodoxy*. The evangelical movement, on the other hand, emerged in a coalition of seventeenth-century movements stressing live orthodoxy, Puritanism and pietism, which in reaction to sectarian division sought to establish a pandenominational movement of evangelical renewal which was nonseparatist, seeking eventual unity of the body of Christ through the reviving of all denominations from within. The leaders of this movement are familiar names among evangelicals: Richard Baxter, the Mathers, Spener, Francke, Zinzendorf, Wesley, Edwards, Whitefield, Dwight, John Newton, Wilberforce, and Simeon. This movement, which was eventually expressed formally in the Evangelical Alliance, phases in and out in its relationship to confessional orthodoxies: sometimes the latter are allies and components within evangelicalism; at other times they are targets of its prophetic challenge and adversaries of its work. Modern confessional orthodox theologians who believe they own the patent to the title *Evangelical,* and who think of evangelicalism as a sort of federation of separated remnants removed from an apostate church, are seriously out of touch with history.[50]

Leaders who would urge the whole evangelical move-

50. For further analysis of the relationship between classical evangelicalism and confessional orthodoxies, see my "Unitive Evangelicalism," in *Dynamics of Spiritual Life* (Downers Grove, IL: Inter-Varsity Press, 1979).

ment to follow once again the ecclesiological strategy practiced during the Fundamentalist controversy—purging of the ranks by heresy trials, or separation under a new name if this fails—should consider the hard facts of Scripture and history which cast doubt on this course. Scripture makes it clear that God does not remove the prophets and pastors who are His gifts to the church when His people turn away and welcome false leaders. The true shepherds remain to warn against the false ones, even at the risk of their lives. The New Testament records no heresy trials and no ecclesiastical separations. Paul's strategy against the Judaizers was to stay with the sheep and warn against the wolves. John remarks concerning heretics, "They went out from us, but they were not really of us; for if they had been of us, they would have remained with us; but they went out, in order that it might be shown that they all are not of us" (I John 2:19, NASB). Note that John does not say, "We threw them out," or "We went out from them," but "They went out from us." The cure for heresy that Paul recommends is not separation but deeper unity: "He gave . . . evangelists . . . pastors . . . teachers . . . for the equipping of the saints . . . to the building up of the body of Christ; until we all attain to the unity of the faith. . . . *As a result,* we are no longer to be children, tossed here and there by waves, and carried about by every wind of doctrine, by the trickery of men, by craftiness in deceitful scheming; but speaking the truth in love, we are to grow up in all aspects into Him, who is the head, even Christ, from whom the whole body, being fitted and held together by that which every joint supplies, according to the proper working of each individual part, causes the growth of the body for the building up of itself in love" (Eph. 4:11–16, NASB).

Pragmatically speaking, there is an important role which confessional orthodox evangelicals can play by following the strategies of purging or separation. As we have indicated, it is often necessary for a group of Christians to purge or to separate in order to become sufficiently disengaged from error to preserve a pure standard of truth in at least one part of Christ's body. But purging and separation have not been the normal course within the evangelical movement, which has characteristically sought the cure for doctrinal weakness in union, not in division. Let us not forget that the magisterial Reformers did not separate, they were ejected, and prevented from reentry except at the cost of vital truth. The events of the early twentieth century indicate that the judicial trials and separations of the Fundamentalists may actually have hurt the cause of the gospel in the larger denominations, and helped precipitate the movement of the children of evangelicals in a liberal direction. We should be alert to the fact that the arguments for limited inerrancy are quite plausible if one fails to read the other side, and that one way to get our children to avoid reading the other side is to start making martyrs.

Therefore, unity, not division, is the answer to the struggle over biblical authority among evangelicals. We must all cleave together harder than ever: evangelicals working to preserve the faith in small denominations and those working to spread and deepen the faith in large ones; those who believe the Bible's truth encompasses every factual detail and those who prefer to stress its perfect guidance in faith and practice. The evangelical task is not yet done; the warring tribes of professing Christians are not yet reformed and revived so that they can become one, as Spener predicted they would. We cannot permit the evangelical movement to be either dismantled or divided. Edwards warns that the devil's strategy against a reviving work of God encompasses both the infiltration of its forces with counterfeit Christianity, and the division of its ranks by separation.[51] The evangelical troops who are

---

51. For further analysis see "How Revivals Go Wrong" in *Dynamics of Spiritual Life*.

wavering in the direction of limited inerrancy may be theologically deficient, but they are not counterfeit warriors, and their victories in the church and in the world are quite real. It follows that the devil's main immediate strategy is to divide and conquer, although his ultimate goal may be to attenuate the faith if an urgent, candid dialogue on this issue is not continued. Orthodox hearts ultimately lead to orthodox minds, and the classical position on inerrancy is strong enough to win those hearts over in an ongoing process of loving argument and admonition. To separate is to admit to weakness and insecurity, and to fail to trust the convincing power of the Spirit and the Word.

But this presupposes a union of orthodox hearts: those which are genuinely cleaving to God and other Christians and urgently seeking for truth, not reacting against past traumas. Harold Lindsell cites a letter from a professor who represents a substantial group of younger persons who are almost postevangelicals:

> I almost never use the word "evangelical" to describe my own position—though it may be in the future, as the word gains new connotations, that I will find the word more congenial. . . . I must clearly state that my own agenda within my own constituency has two high priorities: to use whatever influence I may have to encourage a greater sense of social responsibility and to resist the impact of the Evangelical Theological Society's view of Scripture, i.e., of inerrancy . . . in favor of a greater openness to such issues as biblical criticism.[52]

This is very revealing. On the one hand it shows a legitimate reaction against one area of grave weakness in mainline evangelicalism. On the other it shows both a determined effort to subvert the doctrine of total inerrancy and a spirit of reactive resentment that reflects past wounds at

52. Lindsell, *Battle for the Bible,* p. 128.

the hands of orthodox brethren. Evangelicals who hold to total inerrancy are under no obligation to hire a teacher (or professor) who intends to undermine their teaching in an institution focused on the task of theological training, nor are they under obligation to send him students. They are, however, obligated to empathize and understand the reasons for this reaction and respond with patience, love, and confession (where this is appropriate), seeking the truth in love and rebuking in a spirit of meekness. Those who espouse limited inerrancy are likewise responsible before God to respond with empathy for the Schaeffers and Lindsells who cannot conscientiously hire them or send them students, showing respect for the integrity of their critics even if they continue to differ in love.

This underlines the fact that the primary battleground in the struggle over a correct view of Scripture is not the conflict of conceptual positions, but the challenge to keep responding to one another with gracious hearts. The Fundamentalist controversy was lost not for want of good arguments but through lack of grace under pressure. Paul warns us that we will always lose such battles if we fight them by lashing out at flesh and blood instead of dislodging principalities and powers by prayer and by kind argument, "with all lowliness and meekness, with patience, forbearing one another in love, eager to maintain the unity of the Spirit in the bond of peace" (Eph. 4:2, RSV). We must hope that the ultimate effect of the emergence of sharp conflict over this issue will be, as Jacques Maritain would say, "to distinguish in order to unite," rather than a long divergence of Christians from one another in a graceless chain of polarizations.

Postscript

Recently Harold Lindsell published a sequel to *The Battle for the Bible* in which he suggests that although some individuals may recover their full orthodoxy after losing faith in the total inerrancy of Scripture, institutions almost never do so. He concludes that perhaps those who hold to total inerrancy should simply abandon the term *evangelical* to those who hold a looser position, and refer to themselves as "Fundamentalists" or "Orthodox Protestants."

These suggestions indicate that Lindsell's concept of "evangelicalism" identifies the movement with a federation of groups committed to various confessional orthodoxies (Reformed, Lutheran, and so forth), and does not see it also as a movement designed to be a renewing force, spiritually and theologically, within the mainline churches. Mainline renewal groups contain some leaders who affirm total inerrancy, but also many who (at least for the moment) since 1976 have moved somewhat away from the Hodge-Warfield position. Within these groups, however, leaders on both sides of this issue feel themselves united by so deep an underlying spiritual affinity and so many common goals that they are refusing to abandon the word *evangelical,* under which they have joined to fight the forces opposing biblical Reformation orthodoxy. And they are not eager to revert to the label of "Fundamentalism," which has many negative connotations in the churches they are seeking to reach and renew.

Lindsell's hypothesis that institutions are unrenewable implies that those who stay with the mainline churches, working for their renewal, are wasting their time, since these churches will never return to a broad affirmation of total inerrancy and thus to theological sanity. This seems to suggest a very low estimate of the force of the argument for total inerrancy, and also of the power of Christ to build and restore His church, despite its weakness through sin. Actually, as part of their commitment to theological pluralism within the boundaries of faith in Jesus Christ as divine Lord and Savior, mainline churches today are welcoming the contributions of leaders affirming total scriptural inerrancy. Only those on the right or on the left who refuse to respect and affirm others holding differing theories of biblical infallibility, who work to undermine politically rather than to confront in the arena of theological dialogue, are likely to encounter resistance. Where a high view of Scripture is advanced with intelligence and grace, and accompanied by the fruits of the Spirit, it commands respect and can gain allegiance.

Lindsell's postulate of irreversible decline has been called the "gas bag theory," since balloons collapse readily after one puncture. Our study of history indicates that punctures can come in more than one place in the theological fabric. A rigid, graceless orthodoxy which gives lip service to Christ and Scripture while failing to abide in Christ and to experience the realization of His Word in Christlike behavior may be more resistant to reform and renewal than other movements which are spiritually vital but defective in a few points of theology. An imperfectly managed battle for total inerrancy can, ironically, achieve the reverse of its goal; Fundamentalism was far too successful in the creation of antifundamentalists. Christians are constantly liable to fall away from grace either into heterodoxy or ugly forms of orthodoxy. It would be tragic if the struggle to secure faith in total inerrancy were to become a magic wand with the ability to turn a basically healthy Christian movement into opposing teams of Pharisees and Sadducees.

A gas bag, of course, has no recuperative powers. But the Christian movement is not an inanimate object; it is the body of Christ, and bodies can repair themselves after being wounded. Lindsell implies that the body of Christ suffers from theological hemophilia: if it is wounded, it must bleed to death. I suggest that even a serious theological wound can be healed if the body is cared for in the manner Paul suggests in the fourth chapter of Ephesians.

J. RAMSEY MICHAELS

2

Inerrancy or Verbal Inspiration? An Evangelical Dilemma

A Catchword for Evangelicalism

When a religious or political movement seeks to establish for itself an identity, slogans and rallying cries begin to take on a crucial importance. Their function is to wrap up in a single word or phrase as much of the distinctiveness of the movement as possible, and use it to reinforce the group's identity, both for the benefit of its own adherents and to send a message to the larger public. Something like this has happened with evangelicalism in America in the last generation or so. The evangelical movement during this period represents the coming of age of American Fundamentalism. It has been characterized by an intellectual awakening not only in biblical and theological areas, but also in relation to the broader currents of scientific, cultural, and political thought in the American universities. It has fostered on a rather wide front a reaction against the legalism, separatism, and political quietism of its Fundamentalist past. As they became more intellectually (and socially) respectable, evangelicals cultivated more and more openness to those who did not share all their presuppositions—theological liberals, political activists, Roman Catholics, ecumenical churchmen from many traditions, and minority and Third World groups.

This openness made it all the more necessary for evangelicals to consolidate their own sense of identity. What was it that they in particular had to bring to these dialogues with the wider community? Surely not the Christian gospel as such; only a Fundamentalist would be so bold as to pretend that he had a monopoly on that. Nor were there any ecclesiastical or denominational distinctives that could serve as a banner around which evangelicals could unite. To press strongly for a particular view of baptism or the Lord's Supper was as much of an embarrassment to the cause as quarreling over the millennium or the six days of creation. Evangelicals had been so burned by the divisiveness of Fundamentalism that matters about which they themselves were divided were often because of that very fact judged to be peripheral and secondary. The result was that evangelicalism, in spite of its broadening tendencies, allowed its identity to rest on a very narrow base—the doctrine of Scripture. Even Fundamentalism had appealed to five "fundamentals," but evangelicals distinguished themselves from their fellow Christians almost exclusively by the way they viewed the Bible.[1] This was true even though they remained staunchly faithful to what they considered to be the historic orthodoxy of the church. Other Christians (e.g., many Lutherans, some Anglicans, and the more conservative followers of Karl Barth) maintained these traditional beliefs, but because of their doctrines of Scripture never acquired the label *evangelical*. It was deemed insufficient simply to affirm the authority of the Bible, or to acknowledge it to be the Word of God.

1. Cf. Clark Pinnock, "Three Views of the Bible in Contemporary Theology," in *Biblical Authority*, ed. Jack Rogers (Waco, TX: Word Books, 1977), p. 60; also Bernard Ramm, "Is 'Scripture Alone' the Essence of Christianity?" ibid., p. 112.

Such views were still shared (despite all the inroads of biblical criticism) with large segments of the Christian church. Instead, evangelicalism kept alive the Fundamentalist view of Scripture as the verbally inspired and infallible, or inerrant, Word of God. Although great care was taken to distinguish this view from dictation theories which allowed no significant human activity at all in the writing of Scripture, this was largely the mere disposal of a straw man; few self-respecting Fundamentalists had put much stock in the dictation theory anyway. As one who attended a Fundamentalist seminary in the fifties, and has taught in an evangelical seminary in the sixties and seventies, I have perceived no appreciable differences over Scripture between the two movements. No differences, that is, at the rhetorical level, the level of pronouncements made by churchmen, professors, or journalists who claimed in some way to speak for the wider constituency.

At the grassroots level, it is quite another matter. Most evangelicals who teach the Bible at the college and seminary level have made their peace with biblical criticism to a degree that was never possible in the older Fundamentalism. Careful attention has been given not only to biblical languages and the historical-grammatical understanding of what the biblical texts say, but to hermeneutics, that is, the attempt to translate the biblical message into categories which address today's questions and concerns. This has led to a disinterest in prooftexting and a candid acknowledgment that priority has been assigned to some aspects of the biblical revelation over others. It has also fostered attempts to distinguish critical theories about the Bible which are arbitrary and speculative from those which genuinely illumine our understanding of how God's Word took shape in history.[2] Academic concerns of this kind, for precise

2. This is illustrated most clearly in the writings of F. F. Bruce, who has gained almost universal respect among evangelicals and authority as a spokesman for evangelical biblical scholarship in the academic community at large. Because of him and others like him, such "critical" theories as the use of Mark's Gospel by

definitions and careful distinctions, for sensitivity to nuances and necessary qualifications, do not lend themselves to good sloganeering. Slogans by their very nature simplify, even oversimplify. The danger is that a kind of gap in rhetoric can develop between what evangelical spokesmen say about the Bible and the way in which evangelical teachers and students actually use the Bible.[3] It is not that the two are necessarily inconsistent; it is only that few if any have taken the trouble to show *how* they are consistent.

If one grants the assumption that it is important for evangelicals to maintain a separate and distinct identity within the Christian church, then catchwords such as "inerrancy" are inevitable and necessary. If this separate identity is *not* a crucial concern (a possibility which deserves more consideration than it has received), then evangelicals might safely ignore such slogans and concentrate instead on the more general Christian goals of proclaiming the gospel of Jesus Christ and living as His people in the world—thus losing themselves in the larger body of Christ. At present, however, this second alternative is not a real option for evangelicals in America. Christianity has become such a wide and diverse stream that separate identities within it are necessary in order to preserve what different groups regard as essential aspects of the truth. Historically it was the various denominations which served this purpose, but evangelicalism, like Fundamentalism be-

Matthew and Luke, and their use of another written source ("Q," now lost to us), are as widely accepted by evangelical scholars as by anyone else. In fact, most recent efforts to question or overturn this scholarly consensus have come from *outside* the evangelical camp. Some other views held by Bruce (e.g., two Isaiahs and a late date for Daniel) have made little or no impact on evangelicals, even though his scholarship and orthodoxy remain unquestioned among them. The dynamics of how traditional views change within a confessing community is obviously a complex subject and one that lies outside the scope of this essay.

3. This gap is the subject of Harold Lindsell's *Battle for the Bible* (Grand Rapids: Zondervan, 1976), and can be seen as well in the discussion which this book has generated.

fore it, cut boldly across denominational lines in order to constitute another kind of interest group. For good or ill, evangelicals have themselves become a quasi denomination, with their own leaders, publications, schools and seminaries, and even their own parachurch structures. Within the church they have formed a collective caucus representing a more specific doctrinal commitment, at the one point of Scripture, than have their own respective denominations. Evangelicalism is a unique phenomenon in the church, and as long as it exists, a banner is needed around which to rally. Given this inevitability of slogans, or catchwords, the question is what slogans should be used and how should they be understood, whether within or outside the camp.

It has been my impression that the rallying cry of the Fundamentalism of a generation ago was "verbal inspiration," while the rallying cry of present-day evangelicalism (or at least of its self-appointed spokesmen) is "inerrancy." The former term is seldom heard today (probably because of the bugaboo about dictation theories); the latter was used by Fundamentalists, but much less significantly than in contemporary discussions.[4] It is not my contention that the intended meaning of the two terms was basically any different, although there was, as we shall see, a shift in emphasis. Certainly the impression made on the wider community by the two terms was much the same. But I do suggest that the Fundamentalists were on the better track at this point. *Verbal inspiration* is a term intrinsically better

---

4. As a purely personal, but not untypical, illustration, I have before me two pamphlets by a former professor of mine, the dispensationalist theologian Alva J. McClain: "The Inspiration of the Bible" and "The 'Problems' of Verbal Inspiration." Both were published by the Philadelphia School of the Bible, the former in 1924 and the latter in 1925. I have not found the words *inerrant* or *inerrancy* in either pamphlet, but rather *inspiration, verbal inspiration,* and *infallibility.* David Hubbard notes with surprise that "inerrancy" is missing from the doctrinal statement of the Moody Bible Institute (the words used are, "verbally inspired by the Holy Spirit"). See "The Current Tensions: Is There a Way Out?" in *Biblical Authority,* p. 179.

suited to expressing a viable doctrine of Scripture than is the term *inerrancy.* Whether or not it is the *best* term is another question, and one that lies outside the scope of this essay.

False Issues

Before assessing the respective strengths and weaknesses of "inerrancy" and "verbal inspiration," it is necessary to dispose of several false issues which have played too large a part in previous discussions. For example, it has been objected that inerrancy is unsatisfactory because it is a negative term; it tells what the Bible is not, rather than what it is.[5] But surely this is in the great tradition of the church. The major Christological confessions have focused to a considerable degree on the negative (e.g., "in two natures, inconfusedly, unchangeably, indivisibly, inseparably . . .")[6] in order to preserve the element of mystery in our apprehension of the reality of Christ. There is no reason why we may not be similarly incomplete in what we say about Scripture. Even though Scripture is directly accessible to us in a way in which Christ is not, to speak of it as a revelation from God is to confess a mystery. That we leave a great deal more to be said when we speak of the Bible as inerrant is therefore not necessarily surprising or inappropriate.

Another objection is that when the word *inerrancy* is used without qualification, the assertion made is far too sweeping. Some believe that it should be applied only to what Scripture teaches on questions of faith and practice, not to scientific or historical matters. This approach has

---

5. See, e.g., Berkeley Mickelsen, "The Bible's Own Approach to Authority," in *Biblical Authority,* p. 87.

6. Philip Schaff, *The Creeds of Christendom* (Grand Rapids: Baker Book House, 1977 reprint), vol. II, p. 62.

some plausibility because of the time-honored use of the term *error* to denote false teaching. To say that the Bible is inerrant could therefore mean simply that it teaches no heresy. But in a tradition in which the Bible is itself the standard of true teaching, it is redundant to say that it teaches nothing false. Moreover, those who adopt this approach often create a confusion by the use of the term *limited inerrancy.*[7] Advocates of inerrancy in the usual sense respond quite rightly that "limited inerrancy" is a contradiction in terms. Better to drop a word altogether than qualify it in a way which cancels its meaning.[8] They could have added that, contrary to what was being proposed, "inerrancy" is actually *better* suited, on basis of common usage, to historical and scientific matters than to matters of faith and practice. By drawing attention to the former, and thus virtually challenging skeptics to look for historical or scientific mistakes in the Bible, the term *inerrancy* may in fact be putting the emphasis precisely where it does not belong. Those who adopt so-called limited inerrancy would be better advised, it appears, to point out this danger and instead, with the Westminster Confession, speak of the infallible "rule of faith and life,"[9] thus taking their stand explicitly *against* those who insist on inerrancy as the evangelical rallying cry.[10] Such an approach would maintain a consistency and honesty in the use of language

---

7. See, e.g., R. J. Coleman, "Reconsidering 'Limited Inerrancy,'" *Journal of the Evangelical Theological Society* (*JETS*) 17 (1974), pp. 207–14.

8. See, e.g., J. B. Payne, "Partial Omniscience: Observations on Limited Inerrancy," *JETS* 18 (1975), pp. 37–40; V. S. Poythress, "Problems for Limited Inerrancy," *JETS* 18 (1975), pp. 93–103; Clark Pinnock, "Limited Inerrancy: A Critical Appraisal and Constructive Alternative," in *God's Inerrant Word,* ed. J. W. Montgomery (Minneapolis: Bethany Fellowship, 1974), pp. 143–58.

9. Schaff, *Creeds,* vol. III, p. 602.

10. For an argument that the Westminster divines did not teach the inerrancy of Scripture in the modern Fundamentalist-evangelical sense, see Jack Rogers, "The Church Doctrine of Biblical Authority," in *Biblical Authority,* pp. 17–46. It is curious that many modern advocates of inerrancy who disagree with Rogers' analysis nevertheless regard the Westminster statement as less than adequate for their purposes today.

and would give some indication of where the issue is drawn in the evangelical community. But to object to the term *inerrancy* because it makes an assertion about the whole of Scripture rather than only some parts of Scripture is misguided. Because of its commitment to the canon, whatever the church confesses about the Bible must be something which is applicable to the *whole* Bible—whether the term be "inerrant," "true," "authoritative," "inspired," or merely "worthwhile."

With regard to "verbal inspiration," I have already suggested that those who reject this term out of fear of mechanical dictation theories are on the wrong track. I have never met anyone who held such a theory, and I suspect that (in the twentieth century at least) such a concept exists only so that evangelicals can use it to explain to questioners what their doctrine of Scripture is *not.* Another objection which is still heard, even though it has been answered again and again, is that while the ideas or concepts of the Bible are inspired, it is inappropriate to speak of its actual words as coming from God. The usual answer is the right one: ideas can be expressed only with words.[11] If the concepts are from God, the words cannot be a matter of indifference. Although it is fitting to speak of the Word of God in the words of human beings, these human words are the words which God has *chosen.* Precisely in this way and not in another, He has said what He wants to say. And in any case, it would be incorrect to call the Bible a book of inspired *ideas.* It is a book of words, not just concepts or ideas, and the words form themselves into far more than simply ideas, for example, into stories, events, symbols, visions, songs, poems, feelings, genealogies, liturgies, and much more.[12] To talk of inspired

11. See McClain, "The Inspiration of the Bible," pp. 14ff.; see also Clark Pinnock, *Biblical Revelation* (Chicago: Moody Press, 1971), pp. 89f.

12. Only if "idea" or "concept" is defined so broadly as to include all these varied forms is it permissible to speak of the Bible as a book of ideas. But

ideas is to make of the Bible something different from, and less than, what it really is. Inspiration must be verbal inspiration, and like inerrancy it must be applied, if at all, to the whole of Scripture, that is, it must be what theologians have traditionally called plenary inspiration.

Problems with the Term "Inerrancy"

Once these false issues have been disposed of, it is necessary to take a closer look at the respective merits of "inerrancy" and "verbal inspiration," and especially the very real limitations of the former. The most obvious weakness of the term *inerrancy* is that it blurs the distinction between error and falsehood. An error is a mistake. When a writer makes an error, he fails in some way to realize his intention. But a liar usually says just what he intends to say; he realizes his intention even though the intention itself is immoral. If he does make an error, he is to that extent a poor liar. Thus an inerrant book, technically speaking, may be full of lies. This objection is not as pedantic as it sounds, because for those who insist on inerrancy the bottom line is frequently the slogan, "God doesn't lie."[13] Advocates of the term *inerrancy* actually mean by it, "without error or falsehood," a meaning which is possible only because of a tacit combination of the idea of historical or scientific exactitude with the traditional Christian understanding of error as false or heretical *teach-*

---

concepts or ideas are usually defined more narrowly as rational, often abstract, propositions about reality. The latter definition is in view, for example, in Norman Perrin's recent argument that the kingdom of God is not a concept but a symbol (*Jesus and the Language of the Kingdom* [Philadelphia: Fortress Press, 1976], pp. 33f.).

13. See, e.g., Lindsell, *Battle for the Bible*, p. 182; Pinnock, *Biblical Revelation*, p. 79; R. C. Sproul, "The Case for Inerrancy: A Methodological Analysis," in *God's Inerrant Word*, p. 257.

ing.[14] The fuzzy amalgamation of these two distinct concepts in a single word necessarily leads to confusion. If we want to say "without error or falsehood," then we should say it, and not try to make one word do service for both ideas.

A second objection to the term *inerrancy* is one we have alluded to before. It is that "inerrancy" can be an appropriate category to use in describing historical narrative, or (in a different sense) theological and ethical teaching, but not so appropriate in connection with other genres. What, for example, is inerrant poetry? The Psalms, and much of the other Old Testament wisdom literature, are poetry, as are many passages in the prophets. What exactly does "inerrancy" mean when applied to them? Biblical poetry, like other poetry, is richly expressive of feelings: hope, despair, joy, or anger. How can a feeling be errant or inerrant? Without settling in advance the question of whether there is fiction in the Bible, it is legitimate to ask whether fiction can in any way be equated with error. For example, *if* those scholars are right who have considered Job and Esther to be works of fiction, does that mean that these are somehow works of error or falsehood? A literary critic, in reviewing the latest John Updike novel, would hardly level the criticism that what the author wrote was in error or never happened. He would know that Updike intended to write fiction and not history, and would evaluate him according to his intentions. A novel cannot be errant or inerrant. It may be true or false, but in a quite different sense. "True" in such a context does not mean factual, but authentic, or faithful to human experience or behavior; "false" in the same context does not mean inaccurate or inexact, but unreal, or artificial, or untrue to the author's vision of existence. What does "inerrancy" mean when applied to the parables of Jesus? That He really spoke them? That they must be regarded as stories that actually

14. Cf. G. C. Berkouwer, *Holy Scripture* (Grand Rapids: Wm. B. Eerdmans, 1975), p. 181.

happened? That they provide a true vision of the kingdom of God? It is all left very ambiguous. The point is that the term *inerrancy* (or *errancy* for that matter) is simply not applicable to much that is in Scripture. By clinging to that word, we give the impression that all Scripture is a kind of quasi history, whether its real form is poetry, prophecy, law, proclamation, apocalypse, wisdom sayings, or whatever. The danger is that we run roughshod over the actual phenomena of Scripture in all their formal diversity. The term *inerrancy* thus suffers from significant limitations. It is applicable only to parts of the Bible, not because the other parts contain errors but simply because "error" (or absence of the same) is a meaningless category when applied to certain biblical forms and genres.

The third and most serious objection to the term *inerrancy* centers on its ambiguity. How exactly is it to be defined? Presumably the assertion that a document is without error presupposes some objective standard against which an error is to be measured. An error is a deviation from some norm, but in the case of Scripture, what is the norm? The traditional Christian answer is that the only norm of truth is God Himself. Truth is what God reveals, whether in nature or history or the Bible. There is no standard outside of Him by which the truth or falsity of His revelation can be assessed. It has also been traditionally agreed that His supreme and final revelation is the Bible itself.

Within such a framework, biblical inerrancy can mean only that God has revealed to us in Scripture exactly what He wanted to reveal, no more and no less. This is essentially the understanding of inerrancy which is presupposed in the "Dogmatic Constitution on Divine Revelation" of the Second Vatican Council of the Roman Catholic Church: "Therefore, since everything asserted by the inspired authors or sacred writers must be held to be asserted by the Holy Spirit, it follows that the books of Scripture must be acknowledged as teaching firmly, faithfully, and without error that truth which God wanted put into the sacred writings for the sake of our salvation."[15] The point at issue here is *not* the last phrase, "for the sake of our salvation." Presumably the whole Bible is given for that purpose. It is possible that some of the framers of the document intended the phrase as an expression of a limited inerrancy which distinguishes saving truth from some other kind.[16] But if we leave that phrase aside, we have an eminently satisfactory statement. Another way of saying it is that the Bible affirms without error that truth which God intends to make known, and which we call special revelation.

Inerrancy thus comes to mean simply that the Bible is the Word, or the words, of God. What the Bible says, God says. Inerrancy in this sense really adds nothing to the concept of verbal inspiration. *To call the Bible God's Word and to call it inerrant are not two assertions but one.* Because no one can probe the mind of God directly, such an assertion is not subject to empirical verification or rational demonstration. It can be neither proved nor disproved. A Christian's confidence in Scripture is an a priori commitment of faith, and therefore to the believer not a probability but a certainty. Its basis is not a set of objective data, but what Calvin and others have called the inward testimony of the Holy Spirit.[17] This conclusion, tentative though it is at this stage in the argument, puts me squarely on the side of those whom Clark Pinnock has labeled the *fideists.*[18] For

15. *Documents of Vatican II,* ed. W. M. Abbott (New York: Herder Book Center, 1966), p. 119.

16. See J. W. Montgomery, "The Approach of New Shape Roman Catholicism to Scriptural Inerrancy: A Case Study," in *God's Inerrant Word,* pp. 269f. Cf. also Coleman, "Reconsidering 'Limited Inerrancy,'" p. 209.

17. Cf., e.g., John Calvin, *Institutes* I.7.5; also, E. J. Young as quoted in Pinnock, *Biblical Revelation,* p. 40n.

18. See his discussion in *Biblical Revelation,* pp. 38–44. In this group he includes "Fundamendalists, conservative Calvinists, Neoorthodox loyalists, and post-Kantian liberals" (p. 39), naming such theologians as Calvin, E. J. Young, John Murray, Cornelius Van Til, Herman Bavinck, Abraham Kuyper, Gordon Clark, Karl Barth, and Rudolf Bultmann!

me, the reasoning is simple: if I cannot know God as a direct datum of sense experience, I cannot measure or test the Bible on the basis of how well it agrees with His intentions. All I know of what He intends to say is what I find in Scripture itself. The only exceptions are what theologians have called general revelation and common grace, but these appear not to furnish a sufficiently sturdy platform from which to test the truth or falsity of special revelation.

So we are in a circle—*unless* we shift our ground and make factual correctness (to whatever degree of precision we may choose) the criterion of inerrancy. This is what most modern Protestants have done.[19] Both advocates and opponents of the term *inerrancy* have defined it, without further reflection, as conformity to an external standard of factual accuracy. In this way, for good or ill, they have put it within reach of scholarly proof or disproof. Even some fideists have defined inerrancy in this way while still proposing to defend it on the basis of their faith commitment.[20] It is difficult for me to see how this position can be sustained, for as soon as we speak of facticity, we speak of something which can in many instances be objectively determined, at least with a certain degree of probability, and therefore has to do with more than simply a faith commitment. Therefore most scholars who define inerrancy as factual correctness stress empirical verifiability as the criterion of truth. They comprise the group which Pinnock has called the *revelation empiricists.*[21] Their assumption is that

19. Not so the Roman Catholics. See not only the statement of Vatican II quoted above, but also the article by R. F. Smith on "Inspiration and Inerrancy," in the *Jerome Bible Commentary* (Englewood Cliffs, NJ: Prentice-Hall, 1968), vol. II, pp. 512–14.

20. E.g., Lindsell in *Battle for the Bible,* and E. J. Young in *Thy Word Is Truth* (Grand Rapids: Wm. B. Eerdmans, 1957).

21. *Biblical Revelation,* pp. 44–52. For convenience I will use this term as well, though other terms, such as *Christian rationalist,* are sometimes used. Pinnock includes in this group such conservative theologians as B. B. Warfield, Charles Hodge, C. S. Lewis, John Gerstner, Kenneth Kantzer, Daniel Fuller, John W. Montgomery, and himself, as well as several philosophers of language and Wolf-

God would not reveal something which is not factually accurate. Unfortunately they do not make it clear why this has to be the case, or, if it is the case, what *degree* of exactitude is necessary in order to have something worthy of the divine nature. Are numerical approximations legitimate? Must everything be told in chronological order? Must all conversations be recorded verbatim? Here, as we might expect, the revelation empiricists differ widely among themselves. They do have in common, however, an uneasiness with any notion of taking inerrancy out of the realm of what is empirically and/or rationally demonstrable. To them a view which cannot be proved right or wrong is a view which has no bearing on the real world; if it makes no difference in the sphere of that which can be seen, studied, or measured, it is meaningless. A fideist position, which makes God alone the norm for inerrancy, allows us to assert that what rational inquiry perceives as errors are actually from God. Such "inspired errors," says the empiricist, are sheer nonsense, a contradiction in terms. He says that if they are errors (by his external standard of facticity), they cannot be inspired. The fideist says that if they are inspired, they cannot be errors (in the sense in which *he* has defined error). To the empiricist, the inerrancy (and hence the inspiration) of Scripture is an objective probability; to the fideist its inspiration (or inerrancy) is a subjective certainty.

And so the battle lines are formed. The questions raised by the revelation empiricist are formidable indeed. But what positive alternatives to fideism does he provide? Essentially he imposes on the Bible a standard of truth or facticity external to God Himself, by which God's Word may (indeed must) be judged. In his view, inerrancy is no longer simply another term for verbal inspiration, but in-

---

hart Pannenberg. The prototype, however, is Warfield. See especially his essay, "The Real Problem of Inspiration," in *The Inspiration and Authority of the Bible* (Philadelphia: Presbyterian and Reformed, 1970), pp. 167–226.

stead an *implication* of it, and thus a separate, second assertion brought in alongside the simple acknowledgment that all the words of the Bible are words from God. This second assertion rests on a second standard of truth, that is, *our* concept of objective facticity. But there cannot be two standards of truth. God alone, and what He intends, must be the measure of any inerrancy we confess. Other measures, such as a journalistic accuracy in reporting historical events or discourses, a strict chronological sequence, the absence of outside sources or redaction, numerical exactness, and uniformity of perspective, are based on expectations which *we* bring to the text. They may or may not be part of what God intends. We have no right to assume that what He intended to do is different from what He did do. He has given us a revelation which conforms to our standards of precision only in part. The role of faith is to accept this revelation on His terms, not ours.

In assuming the applicability of his own standards of factual accuracy, the revelation empiricist is actually making certain assumptions about God Himself. Although in most cases he scorns the designation, he is in his own way a presuppositionalist.[22] Like some (though not all) of his fideist colleagues,[23] he argues that because the Bible is God's Word it must *therefore* possess certain qualities which can be known in advance because they mirror the attributes of God Himself, qualities such as unity, self-consistency, and freedom from error. Since God is truth and

---

22. See, e.g., the critique brought by a more consistent revelation empiricist (Daniel Fuller) against a less consistent one (Clark Pinnock) in *Christian Scholar's Review* 2 (1973), pp. 330–33, together with Pinnock's reply. Pinnock virtually acknowledges the point when he speaks of "negative criticism ... beset by the naturalistic presupposition, a condition which prevents it from being truly empirical" (p. 333). Apparently, biblical criticism is "truly" empirical only when it rests on *super*natural presuppositions. What needs to be more clearly stated is exactly what these are.

23. See n. 20, and cf. James Daane's assessment of the similarities and differences between Harold Lindsell and the revelation empiricists ("The Odds on Inerrancy," *Reformed Journal* 26, no. 10 [Dec. 1976], pp. 5f.).

cannot lie, what He reveals must conform to certain standards of truthfulness and factual accuracy. If Scripture is the Word of God, it *must* be inerrant; if it is not inerrant, it can be neither inspired nor authoritative.[24]

The type of fideist position outlined above, on the other hand, is unwilling to decree in advance what God's revelation must or must not be like.[25] It is idle and pointless, after all, to debate theoretically what kind of a revelation God could or would give us when we have right in hand the very revelation which He *did* give us. To find out what inerrancy or verbal inspiration entails, we have only to read it. If we find perfect unity, total self-consistency, and factual precision at every point, so be it. If we find (as we do) a rather complex picture of unity in diversity, relative consistency, and factual agreements and disagreements, the question is whether or not we have a right to say, "God wouldn't do that to us. There must be some other interpretation of these data." This, in effect, is what many Fundamentalists and evangelicals have said,[26] but to say it is to

---

24. Cf. Pinnock, *Biblical Revelation,* pp. 73f. It is noteworthy that the title of Lindsell's book ("the battle for the Bible") appears already in the conclusion of Pinnock's book (p. 228). Ironically, the weapons for Lindsell's "battle" are provided already by the presuppositions of the more cautious and scholarly revelation empiricists from Warfield to Pinnock.

25. Among those fideists whose position on the epistemological question is rather close to that represented in this essay, see E. F. Harrison, "The Phenomena of Scripture," in *Revelation and the Bible,* ed. Carl F. H. Henry (Grand Rapids: Baker Book House, 1958), p. 239; Gerhard Maier, *The End of the Historical-Critical Method* (St. Louis: Concordia, 1977), pp. 71f.; Berkouwer, *Holy Scripture,* pp. 181ff., 241-46, 350-52 and *passim*; Daane, "The Odds on Inerrancy"; Martin Kähler, *The So-called Historical Jesus and the Historic Biblical Christ* (Philadelphia: Fortress Press, 1964), pp. 106-16. What Kähler calls "mediating theology" is the approach of those whom Pinnock designates as the "revelation empiricists," and Kähler's critique of them (pp. 106-13) is well taken. What he calls "Protestant Orthodoxy" (pp. 113-16) is close to the type of fideism represented by Lindsell, Young, and others. Daane's essay is helpful in seeing how much alike these two categories really are.

26. This is implicit in the strong tendencies toward harmonization of difficulties among many defenders of the term *inerrancy.* While it is true that many biblical "discrepancies" are traceable to unwarranted assumptions by modern

back away from our unconditional commitment to Scripture as a Word from God. It is not our place to lay down conditions on the basis of which the Bible may or may not be God's Word.

Almost from the beginning, the Christian church has had to cope with a harmonistic mentality which thought it knew better than God what His revelation should look like. Ever since Tatian in his second-century *Diatessaron* merged the four Gospels into one continuous and harmonious account, well-meaning Christians have tried to improve on the Word of God. The great danger that the revelation empiricist faces is that in his attempts to "defend the Bible" he will find himself actually defending a unified, logical, self-consistent structure of his own making. The non-Christian empiricist, who does not share his a priori faith in a particular concept of God, is often at a loss to correlate this structure with the phenomena which he himself perceives in Scripture. Nor will it do to say that "his eyes are blinded by unbelief," especially after the revelation empiricist has invited the skeptic to examine the evidence for himself and make up his own mind. When the evidence leads the skeptic to a contrary verdict, it is hardly fair to change the rules of the game. When belief and unbelief perceive even the most basic and literal facts differently, apologetics is no longer possible.

The Christian apologist who makes inerrancy subject to empirical verification has taken on himself an intolerable burden. The non-Christian rationalist has only to demonstrate one "error" or apparent contradiction, and the

---

readers, there are others which cannot be eliminated except by a great deal of special pleading. *It is never wrong to reserve judgment on such questions,* but it is easier to do this if we have not insisted too strongly that reason is our arbiter of truth. Rigorous harmonization can very easily become self-defeating, as in the case of J. M. Cheney. In attempting to harmonize the Gospel accounts of Peter's denial, he leaves us with the impression that *all four* Gospels are in error: Peter really denied Jesus *six times!* See Lindsell (who agrees with Cheney), *Battle for the Bible,* pp. 174ff.

whole structure comes tumbling down, at least in his eyes. The apologist then becomes like the legendary Dutch boy trying to plug the leak in the dike with his finger—but with a less happy conclusion! The task he set for himself is hopeless, and he can succeed only by shifting his ground. Though he pays lip service to objectivity and an empirical-rational method, there is in fact no evidence that will ever convince him of an error.[27] All his conclusions are screened through the grid of his presuppositions about the nature of God. He accepts reason when it helps his case, but retreats to a more fideistic stance when the going gets rough.[28] At heart he is a presuppositionalist. His mistake does not lie in his retreat to fideism at the end, but in his pretense that reason has been his guiding principle all along. Reason and empirical evidence will vindicate the *general* reliability of the Scripture, but not the absolute inerrancy which has been the subject of his rhetoric.[29] When he is closely pressed by the skeptic, his initially bold claims will "die the death of a thousand qualifications." The fideist is on much better ground in claiming only that the Scriptures in their entirety are a revelation from God. When empirical evidence supports their factual accuracy, he is interested and pleased; but when it does not or when

27. See, e.g., the stringent requirements laid down by B. B. Warfield in order for a biblical difficulty to be considered an error ("The Real Problem of Inspiration," pp. 217ff.). On such a basis, what error could ever be even tentatively established?

28. See n. 22. Much of the evangelical criticism of Daniel Fuller's position stems from his unwillingness to make such a retreat.

29. Efforts to establish inerrancy in a rigorously logical or empirical way are convincing only to those who need no convincing in the first place! Warfield ("The Real Problem of Inspiration," pp. 201–08) could do so only by arbitrarily abstracting the Bible's teaching about itself (e.g., II Tim. 3:16) from the rest of the phenomena of Scripture. The problems with this approach are: (a) there is no basis in Scripture itself for such a distinction; and (b) "the Bible's teaching about itself" is never precisely that, but rather a claim made by one biblical writer on behalf of *other* portions of Scripture (e.g., Paul on behalf of the Old Testament [II Tim. 3:16]; or Peter on behalf of Paul [II Peter 3:15]). For a recent restatement of Warfield's argument, cf. Sproul, "Case for Inerrancy," pp. 248–60.

it is unclear, his faith is not shaken because he never pretended in the first place that God's revelation had to match perfectly his own expectations or standards of truth.

Thus the major problem with the word *inerrancy* is that it has to a considerable degree been preempted by the revelation empiricists, and in fact lends itself rather well to the meaning which they have placed upon it. When the word is used, it inevitably conveys the impression that the Bible's accuracy can and should be tested by a standard external to itself. More than that, it is a virtual challenge to the skeptic to do so, and to find an error if he can. But if reason and empirical evidence can vindicate the truth of Scripture, they can overturn it as well. In the minds of many scholars, they have done so again and again. If the revelation empiricist is going to be consistent and honest, he will have to hold open the possibility that errors may yet be discovered in his holy book, and his faith shaken by new evidence. His faith has an objective basis, to be sure, but it is only an objective *probability,* and there is always the chance that the odds may be changed by what the scholars find.[30] When this uncertainty is coupled with the fact that the inerrancy he so insistently affirms has to do with original autographs he has never seen, it becomes clear that his faith rests on a somewhat weak foundation.

The advantage of the term *verbal inspiration* is that it is instead pointed in a Godward direction. It affirms that the Bible in its totality and in all its parts comes from God, and expresses word for word what He intends to say. This affirmation can no more be tested empirically than can our confession of the Triune God. It is something which faith recognizes as the witness of the Holy Spirit within and among those who believe. It is part and parcel of what we acknowledge when we respond in faith to the proclamation of the gospel and the teaching of the church. There

---

30. Cf. Daane, "The Odds on Inerrancy."

can be no objection to the term *inerrancy* as long as it is used simply as a synonym for verbal inspiration. But when it becomes (as it does for many modern evangelicals) a *second,* somehow "higher" or more orthodox characterization of the Bible, its value becomes questionable. Imagine someone saying, "*First,* the Bible is a verbally inspired revelation from God, and *second,* it is also factually exact and without error"—as if God were grateful to have our seal of approval on His work! When we have made the first assertion, we have said all that needs to be said. The second assertion is not only anticlimactic, but is something beyond our power to determine with absolute certainty, given the limited tools at our disposal. All we can do is describe and analyze the data of Scripture, interpret the Word of God, and bring it to bear on our varied life situations. It is our calling neither to question nor to defend, but to understand and obey.

The Role of Reason

The preceding arguments may sound to many readers like irrationalism, a plea for blind faith.[31] But my intent is not to reject reason or empirical evidence, only to assign them their proper place. The function of reason in relation to the Bible should not be to assess the ultimate validity of its claims to truth, but rather to discern the form and understand the content of the biblical revelation once its truth has been accepted by faith. The Spirit bears witness to Scripture as the Word of God, and faith responds to this witness, but it remains for reason to determine how this revelation took shape in history and as a body of literature.

31. It has been said to me: "On that same basis someone could equally well accept the Koran, or the Book of Mormon!" The appropriate answer is, "Of course he could. After all, millions do." But the subject of this essay has not been the question of why one should choose Christianity over other options, but how those who are already Christians should regard the Bible.

When it comes to *interpretation,* the fideist must become an empiricist and a rationalist. This means that the so-called historical-critical method is both legitimate and necessary, despite its undeniable misuse by some scholars both past and present.[32] When the conclusions of higher criticism are rejected, it should be because they have violated the canons of good historical method, not because they conflict with a set of philosophical presuppositions. The revelation empiricist often puts himself in the curious position of deciding ultimate questions of truth on the basis of human reason, and then attempting to do his biblical criticism by faith! It has to be the other way around. Reason fulfills its proper function at a second stage, *after* faith has made its commitment to the Bible as God's verbally inspired Word. The role of reason is the same here as in everyday life: to hear and comprehend what has been said and to think through its implications.

This second stage is the focus of my own calling as a New Testament scholar. These reflections thus represent for the most part an excursion out of my immediate field of interest and expertise in order to speak to more basic questions usually addressed by theologians and philosophers. They arise out of a need for a theology of Scripture which affirms without question the full authority and inspiration of the Bible while at the same time preserving my right as a biblical scholar to be honest with the text, to let it be what it is and say what it says. Then, if I do slip into dishonesty or special pleading about the meaning of a text, it is my own blunder, and not something which has been made inevitable by my presuppositions.

Like most of my colleagues in a confessional tradition, whether evangelical Protestant or Roman Catholic, I can live with the term *inerrancy* or *verbal inspiration* or *infallibil-*

---

32. The major flaw in the recent work of Maier (*End of the Historical-Critical Method*) is that he confuses the historical-critical method *as such* with its abuse by certain of its practitioners.

ity. In fact, I have lived with all of them for quite some time. But no one likes to have the terms he uses preempted by spokesmen whose assumptions are alien to his own. Sometimes it is necessary to say more precisely what we mean by the terms we use. Here is one vote for the "verbal inspiration" of my Fundamentalist past over the "inerrancy" of my evangelical present.

ROGER NICOLE

3

The Nature of Inerrancy

Few areas in theology can be considered so plain and self-evident that little danger of deviation exists. In most cases, the path of soundness lies between two abysses, somewhat as a ridge on a steep mountain. Deviation to the right and deviation to the left need alike to be carefully avoided, even though the footing on the ridge itself is not always easy. Surely, this kind of situation is well illustrated in Christology, where the church learned, sometimes through painful losses, that it must maintain the full deity and the full humanity of Jesus Christ and acknowledge these as conjoined in the most intimate manner in the unity of His person. The subject of the inspiration of Scripture also falls in this category. Here it is essential to affirm the divine authorship of the Bible with all that this involves concerning the character of the product, and at the same time to recognize the reality of the contribution of the human authors, who were not used as robots or computers, simply to register mechanically some input placed into them by God, but who were commissioned to be the bearers of the divine Word in full keeping with their background, culture, personal training, language, and individuality. How these two can be combined remains a mystery to us. Yet the point of view that fails to do justice to both elements is bound to be an inadequate expression of the biblical doctrine of inspiration. Unfortunately, too many people have allowed themselves to move into areas of danger in which the truth of one or the other side was jeopardized. Sometimes, especially when logic has been permitted to have its full sway, this has taken them down into the abyss. Their downfall must stand as a warning to others.

Similarly, when we consider the topic of inerrancy, we must be wary of abysses lying on either side of us. On one side, there are those who, apparently in order to safeguard the human element involved in the writing of the Scripture, have thought it necessary to deny that the sacred writers were protected from error in everything they wrote. Those who hold this view sometimes say that the inspired writers were protected from serious error; or again that they were protected from error in matters related to faith and practice, while they remained susceptible to error in other areas; or again that they were free from error in their major message but subject to it in peripheral areas. The problem with this position is that it dilutes the authority of the Scripture and seems to open a way of escape from the impact of this authority, although undoubtedly limitations set upon inerrancy were not intended deliberately as a means to eschew the authority of the Word of God. This position also suffers from a lack of definiteness, so that one is left to his own judgment concerning what is serious error; or again, what relates to faith and practice and what does not relate to them; or again, what is central and what is peripheral. If it is left to the individual's own judgment to determine what is authoritative and what is not, it is obvious that the supreme priority of the authority of Scripture will be damaged.

On the other side, some who have been very resolute advocates of inerrancy tend to provide their own strict definition of inerrancy, a definition often devised in terms of a rationalistic framework. Then they insist that this definition holds for all the phenomena of Scripture. In the process they sometimes press the phenomena of Scripture into conformity with this definition and thus open themselves to the charge of artificiality. Surely, this is not the appropriate way to approach the Scripture. To move along these lines will not do justice to either the Bible or the God of the Bible.

The path of soundness will have to be recognized as falling between these two extremes. Inerrancy must be defined strictly in terms of Scripture's representation of what God is and does. At the same time we should not permit ourselves to entertain a view in which the frailties of the human authors impinge on the veracity of God. The present essay is designed specifically to ascertain the nature of inerrancy by exploring the biblical teaching and phenomena rather than to bring to the Scripture an arbitrary definition or rationalistic expectation concerning what God *should* do.

Areas of Common Misunderstanding

1. The relationship between the autographs and the copies in the original languages

One could argue that if God were supremely interested in inerrancy He would have seen to it that those who copied the text were always infallibly kept from slips by the power of the Holy Spirit. In this case all our manuscripts would be precisely alike and there would be no reason for a science of textual criticism. In fact, however, we do find that manuscripts differ. We find that those ancients who quoted or copied the Bible were subject to the same frailties which are found among those who copied other works. Probably no manuscript is entirely like any other manuscript, for even those who did their labors with painstaking care still introduced some slight deviations into their product. We need to take account of this in our understanding of inspiration. It was recognition of this fact which led evangelical theologians to emphasize the inspiration of the original autographs.[1] Sometimes those who object to the position of the advocates of inerrancy imagine that this qualification was designed to provide a huge loophole in case of serious difficulties that might be encountered in the Bible. Then the advocate of inerrancy could always say, "This was not in the original." While he could not prove it, no one could prove otherwise.

Very definitely this is not the origin or the purpose of distinguishing between autographs and copies. Evangelicals who hold to inerrancy should be very careful not to raise questions rashly in relation to the text when no evidence is available that an error of transmission has in fact occurred. It is true, of course, that we cannot absolutely rule out the possibility of such an error even in the case of a great consensus of the various manuscripts. Yet the very great concurrence of the manuscripts of the Bible gives us strong warrant to rejoice in the assurance that God has safeguarded for us a text which is in substantial conformity

1. B. B. Warfield, *The Westminster Assembly and Its Work* (New York: Oxford University Press, 1931), pp. 236–51; François Turrettini, *Institutio Theologiae Elencticae,* Locus II, Q. X (New York: Carter, 1847), vol. I, pp. 96ff.; Louis Gaussen, *Théopneustie,* 2nd ed. (Paris: Delay, 1842), pp. 241–88.

It is true that in their famous article on "Inspiration" (*Presbyterian Review* 2 [April 1881], pp. 225–60), A. A. Hodge and B. B. Warfield introduced the possibility that an early slip in the transmission of the text may be the source of an apparent error in Scripture (pp. 237, 242). They do this in the process of placing in evidence some considerations which those who would charge the Scripture with error should not be permitted to disregard. But they very seldom have recourse to this explanation as affording the solution of specific difficulties. In the article in question, as a matter of fact, neither of them invokes this as a solution of any of the difficulties which they examine.

with what was originally given.[2] At times in the presence of variants which leave the textual critic in a quandary, we may do well to acknowledge that certainty cannot be reached. Then we may not base any teaching or mandate upon the words which are in question. But in the overwhelming preponderance of cases even the variants that we do have do not impinge on the message of the Scripture, and thus the frailties of man in the process of transmission have not deprived us of the divine authority we need in faith and practice.

It must be understood, however, that inerrancy in the Scriptures does not imply that we must posit a constant miracle in transmission by which anyone who copies, engraves, or quotes the Bible will be forever protected from any kind of slip. Some will wonder: since God has not seen fit to protect His Word in this way, is it important to insist that the Word as originally given was kept immune from all error? To answer this question, remember that the doctrine of inerrancy is inferred from the truth that God is the author of Scripture and that therefore God's veracity applies to the wording of the Bible. It may be helpful at this point to record some considerations which may bring the matter into focus.

a. *The fact that there are various transcriptional forms tends to confirm the reliability of the text in the very many cases where there is overwhelming agreement.* The situation is analogous to that of a series of witnesses in court. The diversity of presentations indicates that no collusion has taken place and that the various witnesses function independently of each other. Similarly, the variety of manuscripts and even of families of manuscripts reinforces our conviction that what

2. This is undoubtedly the meaning of the phrase "by his singular care and providence, kept pure in all ages" (Westminster Confession of Faith, I.8). At times some of the theologians of the seventeenth century did show a certain restiveness in this area, as when they held that the force of the Hebrew vowel points had to be a part of the original deliverance (*Formula Consensus Helvetica,* 1675).

we do have is not a trumped-up text but that the manuscripts in our possession are in fact related closely and vitally to the original. In this regard, our situation with respect to the Old Testament was enhanced by the discovery of the Dead Sea Scrolls. Before that time the extant manuscripts had largely reflected the Masoretic school. Their close resemblance to each other gave us little basis for textual criticism, and a real possibility remained that the original text at some points may have been replaced by something else which the Masoretes favored. The Dead Sea Scrolls are witnesses which antedate much of the Masoretic labors, and, while they introduce at times variant readings, they also substantially confirm the reliability of the text we have used for centuries. The possession of some autographs would, of course, be a boon, but in their absence, the textual variants may serve as a confirmation at most points of the authenticity of what we have.

b. *A slip in the transcriptional process is always subject to human correction.* This is an area in which men are competent to act and to express meaningful opinions. Errors in the original would not similarly respond to treatment by men. The analogy suggested by R. Laird Harris is helpful here. Loss or destruction of the standard yard at the Smithsonian Institution would not enormously affect the practice of measurement in the United States, for a comparison of the multitudinous copies of that yard would lead us to something very close to the original standard. On the other hand, demonstration that the standard itself was not correct would have far-reaching implications for all measurements throughout the country.[3]

c. *Some problems in the transcriptional process were already in existence in the days of our Lord and His apostles; yet they did not hesitate to rely on the authority of Scripture.* Thus it is apparent that sufficient accuracy was present as to permit them to

3. R. Laird Harris, *Inspiration and Canonicity of the Bible* (Grand Rapids: Zondervan, 1957), pp. 88f.

ground their teaching or arguments on what was transcribed.

d. *The possibility of transcriptional errors is not a late discovery,* even though it is only since the development of printing that the full range of possible errors became apparent. As early a writer as Augustine already was aware of the possibility of some flaws in this respect. In fact, he would use this as a possible explanation for some difficulties that he might find in Scripture.[4] Even in his case, however, this was hardly a loophole provided to insure that he would be safeguarded from embarrassment. In his practice as an exegete he scarcely ever suggests that the text was corrupted.

e. *If God had been pleased to preserve some autographs for us, there is reason to believe that some people might have been affected by a superstitious veneration for them.* These people would have viewed the autographs as sacred relics, and a kind of "bibliolatry" might have developed which would have been injurious to the soul. It is interesting that King Hezekiah destroyed the brazen serpent that Moses had made, and was commended for this action (II Kings 18:4).

The Bible has been inspired to provide for us a message relating to spiritual matters and on that account the measure of uncertainty which has been introduced by the presence of variants (e.g., deterioration in minute details; change in word order) does not really impair the authority of the Scripture. It can be said that copies of the Bible are inerrant to the extent that they agree with the original, and by all reasonable constructions, this extent is very considerable. It is so remarkable in fact that, except for inscriptions made on stone or on papyri, we do not have any text of antiquity which appears so well preserved as the Old and New Testaments.

---

4. Augustine, Letter 82.3 (to Jerome), *Nicene and Post-Nicene Fathers,* 1st series, vol. I, p. 350.

It is frequently urged that, since the process of transmission has delivered to us a text which may not be in every respect identical with the autographs, it does not matter very much to us whether the autographs were, in fact, free from error. This point appears to have some force if one looks simply at the character of the text that we possess. But even that force, we trust, is sharply limited by the considerations introduced just above. What seems to elude the mind of those who press the claim is the fact that in the Bible we do not only have a written norm, but we have a claim of divine authorship as well. If the Bible is indeed the Word of God, can it be thought that in its original form it was blemished by numerous errors? A text of Cicero may have reached us with some attrition through the transcriptional process, and this may have damaged its style. But if a claim is made that the inferior character of a text in very poor Latin is an original feature, then the likelihood of Ciceronian authorship is reduced to the extreme. This seems to be the abiding difficulty of those who deny inerrancy. They proffer to us a text which is subject to challenge at some points, and whose authenticity as a divine document is placed in jeopardy by the blemishes which they allege.

2. The process of translation

Some people claim that translation inevitably tampers with an original pronouncement. It is true, of course, that in translation it is very difficult to provide a statement in another language which says absolutely no less and no more than the original and which conveys precisely the same impression to the hearer or the reader. Since most people do not have access to the Bible in the original languages, this may appear very disturbing, for they may fear that the human process of translating has substantially impaired the authority of the original Word of God. But here again the argument appears to raise fears that are not warranted by the facts of the case.

The same formula which we used in relation to textual variants may apply here as well: *Any translation is entitled to acceptance as the Word of God to the extent that it corresponds to the original.* This extent is very considerable for translations executed with appropriate care and without a subtle bias. If anyone should be inclined to interpret the Scripture in some unusual way on the basis of a translation, then he should check with the original to be sure that the meaning which he perceives is, in fact, present in the text. Individuals may easily fall into misunderstanding some portion of Scripture; it should be remembered, however, that the Bible is received from God not to be a strictly private instrument, but to be used and applied in the fellowship of God's people. Thus we can be protected from vagaries by the insights, the wisdom, and the scholarship of our fellow Christians.[5]

It is encouraging in this respect to see that the apostles in the preponderance of cases did not hesitate to use the Septuagint translation when referring in Greek to the Old Testament. Now the Septuagint was far from being a homogeneously excellent translation in terms of modern standards of translating, but it was well known, and was deemed adequate to convey to Greek readers the meaning of the Old Testament Hebrew. Thus we find that under the inspiration of the Holy Spirit the New Testament

5. One should be very careful not to develop this line of approach into a slavish acceptance of tradition, for the Bible must remain the judge of tradition rather than the other way around. In Matthew 15 and Mark 7 our Lord castigated human traditions which had moved far away from the intent of Scripture. He declared, "You nullify the word of God by your tradition" (Mark 7:13, NIV). With due concern not to fall into a similar defect, we should recognize, however, that in the process of interpreting the Scripture, there are great benefits to be derived from a wholesome consideration of what other Christians have understood. If we take care to learn from them, we will not credit at once as God's Word certain eccentric interpretations which arise occasionally, particularly where there is no knowledge whatsoever of the original.

writers did not see fit to make a new authoritative and inspired translation, but they frequently made appeal to the Septuagint as embodying in sufficient manner what they wanted to emphasize. They did not, however, base their argument or their use of the text upon something which might be inferred from the Greek but which could not be found in the Hebrew.[6]

3. Spelling

In modern times certain standards of spelling are established in most languages. It is a part of the equipment of culture to be able to exhibit a reasonable conformity to these standards. An author or a publisher who does not abide by them opens himself to the charge of lacking culture or care. In this connection we often use the expressions "mistakes in spelling" or "spelling errors." It must be noted at once, however, that here we do not have an issue of conformity to or departure from factual truth. In fact,

---

6. It must be recognized that there are some passages where the New Testament writers have been charged with doing precisely that, although this view of their use of the Septuagint is by no means necessary. A passage in point might be Hebrews 10:5, where Psalm 40:6 is quoted as saying, "A body you prepared for me" (NIV). The Masoretic Hebrew reads, "You have opened my ears." Some feel that later in the same context, when the author writes "through the sacrifice of the *body* of Jesus Christ" (v. 10), he is referring specifically to the form of language found in the Septuagint. The possibility does exist that the Septuagint bears witness to another form of the Hebrew text, which may be the original form. The Qumran scrolls have given us some examples of a Hebrew *Vorlage* for the Septuagint text, which some scholars consider as preserving the original form rather than the Masoretic text (e.g., Isa. 53:11). But in any case the author of Hebrews does not press the text of Psalm 40 beyond what could legitimately be inferred from the Masoretic text, for the presence of "ears" surely implies the existence of a "body." Therefore, one cannot maintain that the writer of Hebrews exploited a faulty Septuagint translation to prove something that the Hebrew text could not support. One could go so far as to say that the Masoretic text would be even more appropriate than the Septuagint form in emphasizing the voluntary obedience of Christ, the suffering servant, although this emphasis was not indispensable to the point of the author of Hebrews. This complex subject would warrant a fuller discussion which we do not have the space (nor the ability) to provide here.

appropriate spelling varies from age to age and sometimes from one country to another. For instance, British writers will spell "favor" with a "u" (favour) which American writers omit. Obviously, extreme oddities of spelling might actually becloud a text, but this is a feature which we do not see in the Bible. At the same time, it is not necessary to imagine that the fact of divine authorship made it imperative that God should control the spelling habits of the human writers. Thus, in Matthew 27:46 the cry of dereliction of our Lord appears to have been spelled "Eli"; while in Mark 15:34, we encounter the spelling "Eloi." Here the Gospel writers were concerned to render for us the very sound of the voice of our Lord, but there was no necessity to secure identical phonetic symbols for this purpose. Similarly, many names, particularly those that are transcribed from another language, can be appropriately spelled in a variety of ways. The phenomena of Scripture will lead us to the conclusion that while the spelling practices of the sacred authors did not disfigure the sacred text, God appears not to have been concerned to supervise their handling of this matter as if they were participating in a spelling bee! This should not surprise anyone, since spelling is merely a human convention.

4. Grammar

Grammar may be defined as a codification of the principles generally accepted in the proper usage of a language. It is indispensable for the purpose of communication and here again people of culture will manifest a certain conformity to the usage which is characterized as correct. A complete disregard of rules of grammar breeds ambiguity and in extreme cases opaqueness. We find that the Scripture was not written with such cavalier disregard. Yet there are at times puzzling cases, particularly in the state in which the texts have reached us, where it is difficult to ascertain the precise construction intended by the authors.

It is also a matter of plain fact that they have used various turns of speech which from the point of view of grammar might not appear commendable. We have sentences that are suspended; we have verbs where the subject is in doubt; we have forms of speech which might have fallen under the condemnation of a classical Hebrew or Greek grammarian. There were some scholars in the seventeenth century who imagined that since the Bible is the Word of God, the Hebrew and Greek appearing in it must be deemed the supreme and perfect grammatical form of these languages. This, however, is not the case. Furthermore, there is no uniform standard in the Old Testament or the New. And there is no necessity to consider that the grammar of Koine Greek is lifted up above the usage of Plato and Thucydides.

Here again it must be emphasized that we do not have an area where truth is at stake but merely adherence to a human convention of language. The convention itself fluctuates in both time and space. The biblical writers appear to have been permitted to express themselves in the idiom which was natural to them without receiving a supernatural help that would preclude expressions or turns of phrase that would offend a purist. It is therefore no disrespect to the Word of God to say that the author of Revelation in that book has used a form of Greek which is heavily colored by Hebraisms, expressions that would be rated incorrect in terms of standard Greek grammar.[7]

5. Phenomenological use of language

In our scientific age with the many advances which it has brought us with respect to dissemination of knowledge, access to information, and general acquaintance with scientific concepts, cultured people have developed ways of

7. To give only one example, Revelation 1:4 has ἀπὸ ὁ ὢν, which would be equivalent to "from *he* who is"!

expressing themselves which take account of the best insights of human science. Even so, there are still expressions frequently used which reflect a phenomenological approach to reality. Very few people of culture, for instance, believe that the alternation of day and night is due to the movement of the sun. They realize that this phenomenon is produced by the rotation of the earth around its axis in twenty-four hours, and yet numerous expressions which might seem to imply the opposite are still considered quite appropriate: "the sun goes down," "the sun is high on the horizon," "sunrise," "sunset." The latter two appear even in astronomical publications! These are phenomenological uses of language where events are related from the vantage point of a spectator on the earth who describes what he observes rather than gives an explanation of the process by which the events in view are being caused. This is the situation throughout the Scripture. The Bible was not written in order to promote a particular view in scientific matters. It was meant as an address which would be understandable, regardless of the stance which one takes with respect to certain scientific theories. It is because the theologians of the seventeenth century failed to perceive this that they condemned Galileo. Both they and Galileo should probably have perceived that God was not taking sides in this matter and had not inculcated one particular view in Holy Writ. Warned by this egregious mistake, we should be careful to acknowledge the use of language prevailing at the time of the writing of the various books of the Bible, to accept the descriptions at face value, and not to read into the Scripture a commitment to positions about which the Bible does not give us a divine determination.

6. Approximations

Because of the ready availability of information we often pride ourselves in our day on strict accuracy. Even so, we commonly have recourse to approximations, which are recognized as being legitimate ways of presenting the truth. If someone asks me the population of Boston, I may reply "640,000," which is the nearest figure within 10,000 to the census of 1970. Very few people would expect me to say 641,071. That figure, in fact, would not be meaningful because it would not necessarily reflect the exact population at any one time and particularly not at the time of my answer. Similarly, when people are queried about their age, assuming that they wish to convey truthful information, they do not reply: "32 years, 5 months, 4 days, 2 hours, 52 minutes, and 35 seconds"; but they usually provide an approximate figure simply in terms of years. The integrity of truth is not at stake here. God, who knows all figures without approximation, has nevertheless seen fit to use approximations repeatedly throughout the Scripture. This is undoubtedly the case in all kinds of matters like numbers of people, size of armies, as well as in chronological matters or in measurements. Punctilious accuracy in the scientific sense is obviously not an aim of Scripture. As long as approximations are appropriate, no charge of failure to observe the truth can be leveled.

The same principle would apply with respect to the use of quotations and the relating of statements made in conversation. Our present practice of scholarship has led us to insist on a very high level of accuracy whenever we transcribe the words of another. But we have no ground to insist that this standard must have prevailed in biblical days. Thus we find that the New Testament writers, and presumably our Lord Himself, quoted the Old Testament with a considerable measure of freedom, adapting the words of ancient writers in many cases to the contemporaneous situation. They freely omitted elements which did not appear relevant or inserted words that would elucidate more fully the sense in which they construed the ancient oracle. Similarly, in the four Gospels we have evidence that considerable freedom was used in the reporting of conversations in the days of our Lord. We have no right to posit a procedure which in our judgment the writers of the Bible should have used and then to proceed to judge them in terms of their conformity or lack of conformity to it. We need rather to observe the facts of the situation and to be satisfied with the way in which they were led to make their sacred record. Moreover, it would be wrong to imagine that one writer arbitrarily changed something which he found in another inspired writer on the ground that it did not conform to truth. Those who hold to inerrancy will retain the conviction that a real underlying harmony exists between various accounts which differ somewhat in details.

7. Fragmentary information

It is very important to realize that absolute completeness is not indispensable for truth. If it were, we would despair of ever reaching truth at any point. The fragmentary character of information must be kept firmly in mind in relation to any account. This is the case also with respect to the Scripture. The writers led by God in their sacred writings selected data out of an immense pool of details which could have been given. This principle is specifically asserted in John 20:30, where we read: "Jesus did many other miraculous signs in the presence of his disciples, which are not recorded in this book." And again in John 21:25: "Jesus did many other things as well. If every one of them were written down, I suppose that even the whole world would not have room for the books that would be written" (NIV). The fragmentary nature of the information would encourage us to view the various writings as supplementing each other rather than as falling into a pattern of error due to incompleteness. A fair number of the difficulties that have been raised in relation to the Scriptures may perhaps find a solution when this principle is duly recognized.

8. Lack of uniformity

Because a uniformity of standards frequently prevails in the modern scientific world, we usually expect that a well-written book will follow a uniform standard throughout. But this requirement cannot be placed upon the Scripture; we ought to recognize that varieties of standards may well prevail in measurements, in dating the reigns of kings, and in a number of other areas concerning which the ancient world had no uniform standard. Thus, a cubit may conceivably not mean exactly the same length in Genesis, Ezekiel, and the Book of Revelation. It is also probable that the principles for the dating of the reigns of kings differed in the kingdoms of Israel and Judah.[8]

This does not lead us to the supposition that the biblical writers were permitted to incorporate without correction faulty data which they may have found in extant records, but it does emphasize that we are not in a position to project upon their writings the expectation that in terms of accuracy they will conform to present canons of scientific writing.

9. Etymologies

Biblical etymologies have sometimes given difficulty to linguistic scholars. It is a possibility that it was never intended that we be able to trace the historical origin of certain names appearing in Scripture, as modern etymological science seeks to do. Scripture merely indicates some correspondence between the name of a place and certain important incidents which occurred there, or between the name of a person and a certain divine purpose in that person's life. To accomplish this a mere alliter-

---

8. The brilliant labors of Edwin R. Thiele appear to have established this (*The Mysterious Numbers of the Hebrew Kings,* 2nd ed. [Grand Rapids: Wm. B. Eerdmans, 1965]).

ation is effective, as well as a truly scientific linguistic etymology.

10. Transcendent truths

There are elements of the Christian faith which so far transcend the comprehension of finite minds that it is probably impossible to formulate in terms of our finite perspective a wholly satisfactory rational harmonization of facets of the truth which confront us in the form of paradox or antinomy. By way of examples we might adduce the distinctness and integrity of the two natures in the unity of the person of Christ, or the confluence of the sovereign action of God and of the responsible decisions of rational agents, or again the unity of essence and trinity of persons in the Godhead. Obviously we should never commit the grievous mistake of regarding as error or contradiction in Scripture what simply transcends our finite minds by simultaneously asserting complementary aspects of the truth whose ultimate harmony is perceived in infinity but is not accessible to finite rational investigation.

A Definition of "Inerrancy"

Other aspects of the veracity of the Bible might be investigated, but for the present purposes this will suffice.[9] When the phenomena adverted to above are duly taken in consideration, certain parameters for the meaning of

---

9. Further very helpful elaboration may be found in Robert Preus, "Notes on the Inerrancy of Scripture," *Bulletin of the Evangelical Theological Society* 8, no. 4 (Autumn 1965), pp. 127–38. One should also consult his important chapter on "The Truthfulness of Scripture" in *The Theology of Post-Reformation Lutheranism* (St. Louis: Concordia, 1970), pp. 339–62, 394–400. Of great interest also, although not supporting inerrancy as we view it here, is the article by G. Courtade, "Inspiration et Inerrance," in L. Pirot, *Supplément au Dictionnaire de la Bible* (Paris: Letouzey & Ané, 1949), vol. IV, pp. 482–559.

"error" may begin to appear, parameters established not on the basis of a preconceived opinion as to what the Bible may or may not contain, but at least in good part on the basis of the phenomena manifestly exhibited in the performance of those who wrote. Within this framework it appears possible to assert with confidence the "inerrancy" of the Bible as an inevitable implication of the veracity of God and of the divine authorship of Scripture. Inerrancy will then mean that at no point in what was originally given were the biblical writers allowed to make statements or endorse viewpoints which are not in conformity with objective truth. This applies at any level at which they make pronouncements. Notably, this will serve to corroborate the truth of external sources which they might have used in the preparation of their text and whose data were embodied in the text. Obviously, this does not confer a divine endorsement on all statements made by all the individuals who appear in the drama of the Bible. Surely the words of Satan, the friends of Job, Esau, Pharaoh, Sanballat, and the unbelieving leaders in Palestine in Christ's day do not receive God's approval by the mere fact that they are recorded in Scripture.[10] Similarly, some written documents quoted in Scripture would not necessarily receive divine endorsement.[11] In these cases the inerrancy of Scripture means that the writers of Holy Writ were guided by God to

10. In I Corinthians 3:19 Paul quotes with approval a statement of Eliphaz the Temanite (Job 5:13), but it may well be urged that here Paul does not rely on this statement as a divine authority for asserting the limitations of human wisdom, but simply finds in the ancient text an impressive formulation of that truth, which he adopts for his present purpose. This might well be analogous to certain quotations from extrascriptural sources (cf. Aratus in Acts 17:28, Menander in I Cor. 15:33, and Epimenides in Titus 1:12).

According to John 11:49f. Caiaphas was led to prophesy a truth which transcended what he had consciously in mind. Thus God may at times use even rebellious people to speak His truth, but this does not confer automatic reliability on everything they say! We needed John's comment (vv. 51-52) to be assured about the divine stamp of approval on this utterance of Caiaphas.

11. II Kings 19:10-13; Ezra 1:2-4; 4:11-16, 17-22; 5:7-17; 6:3-12; 7:12-26; and Acts 23:26-30 might be examples in point.

record in a perfectly adequate way what the people in question said or wrote. Throughout history this point was always clear in the mind of wise advocates of inerrancy.[12]

Those, however, who have attempted to expand this principle into the position that God does not vouch for the accuracy of material from other sources which the sacred writers used and transcribed appear to us to dilute the authority of Scripture.[13] If God did not guide the sacred writers in the choice of the material that they decided to incorporate into their own text, then it will be forever impossible to distinguish between what is truly God's Word and what may be simply an accurate record of a fallible source. To the extent that any material appears endorsed by the sacred writer, it must be viewed as endorsed by God as well.

The Problem of Apparent Discrepancies

Some scholars strongly emphasize that the phenomena of Scripture *do* lead us to posit errors of fact, and for this reason these scholars naturally wish to avoid the whole language of inerrancy. Undoubtedly, there are some cases in which the statements of Scripture might appear to fall in this category, and one can easily understand how it might seem more tempting to account for the "error" by assuming an original mistake in a peripheral matter rather than to have to labor to explain away the apparent contradiction between what the Scripture says in one place and other

12. Turrettini, *Institutio,* Locus II, Q. IV, #IV (vol. I, pp. 59f.); R. Pache, *The Inspiration and Authority of Scripture* (Chicago: Moody Press, 1969), pp. 133f.; Tenis Van Kooten, *The Bible: God's Word* (Grand Rapids: Baker Book House, 1972), p. 97; John H. Gerstner, *A Bible Inerrancy Primer* (Grand Rapids: Baker Book House, 1965), pp. 55f.

13. James Orr, *Revelation and Inspiration* (London: Duckworth, 1910), pp. 179–81, 213–15; E. J. Carnell, *The Case for Orthodox Theology* (Philadelphia: Westminster Press, 1959), pp. 102–09; Courtade, "Inspiration," pp. 549–50.

passages of Scripture or some elements of truth that we have culled from other avenues of endeavor. In our judgment this temptation must be resisted, because the assumption that original erroneous material was introduced into Holy Writ jeopardizes both the authority of the Bible as a norm and the divine authorship. Meanwhile, it should be strongly emphasized, as B. B. Warfield has done,[14] that the authority and inerrancy of Scripture are not dependent upon our ability to provide in every case a rational explanation of difficulties encountered. The authority of Scripture is not dependent upon the ability or resourcefulness of any man to vindicate its truth at every point. Therefore, we should never be reluctant to acknowledge that we may not at the present time be in possession of the solution of particular difficulties. This would surely be a wiser course of action, and more conformed to scholarship, than to present a scheme of harmonization that would be so obviously contrived and artificial that those who hear it might gain the impression that we are insincere and that we can hardly entertain seriously the thought that such an explanation is valid. This kind of approach would only promote suspicions concerning our own integrity, and it is surely far better occasionally to acknowledge ignorance, than to incur the distrust of people who will think that we are not dealing squarely with them.[15]

---

14. Warfield, *The Inspiration and Authority of the Bible* (Philadelphia: Presbyterian and Reformed, 1948), pp. 127f., 215f., 219ff., 225, 439. "Our individual fertility in exegetical expedients, our individual insight into exegetical truth, our individual capacity of understanding are not the measure of truth. If we cannot harmonize without straining, let us leave unharmonized" (p. 219). Cf. also James I. Packer, *Fundamentalism and the Word of God* (London: Inter-varsity, 1958), pp. 108f.

15. John Calvin did not hesitate to acknowledge that he was puzzled in the presence of certain difficulties of Scripture. But far from viewing any of these as indicative of a mistake in the original, his language implies precisely the opposite.

In his commentary on Matthew 27:9 he says: "How the name of *Jeremiah*

At times there may be a variety of ways in which a particular difficulty may be resolved, none of which may be so manifestly superior to the others that we are compelled to judge that it must be *the* solution. In such cases it has been a common practice in the history of biblical exegesis to present these various explanations together with their strong and weak points, and to leave it to the reader to decide which one, if any, he prefers. Even if none of the suggestions advanced commends itself at the present time to the point of acceptance, this fact does not constitute an invalidation of the truthfulness of the sacred records, which may be presumed true unless they are so cogently demonstrated to be in error that not only is no acceptable solution presently in view, but no conceivable solution can even be envisioned.[16]

In the wise providence of God many features of Scripture which were very puzzling in previous times received satisfactory explanation when additional knowledge was secured which permitted us to understand better the pur-

---

crept in, I confess that I do not know, nor do I give myself much trouble to inquire. The passage itself plainly shows that the name of *Jeremiah* has been put down by mistake, instead of Zechariah." Here Calvin, perhaps rashly, assumes a textual corruption, the origin of which he does not feel obligated to explain. Similarly in his commentary on Acts 7:14–16 Calvin suggests that the text must be emended. He is unwilling to consider that either Stephen or Luke could have committed a mistake even in small details.

16. Cf. the fine statement by Warfield, *Inspiration and Authority of the Bible*, p. 225. Calvin frequently lists a variety of explanations in his *Commentaries*, sometimes indicating his own preference for one among them. The concern which he shows to provide explanations for apparent discrepancies (e.g., in relation to the raising of Jairus's daughter [Matt. 9:18ff., etc.]; or the healing of the blind near Jericho [Matt. 20:29–34, etc.]; or in the narratives concerning the resurrection of Christ [Matt. 28:2ff., etc.]) manifests clearly that he did not entertain the possibility that the Scripture might be in error. It is strange that some of these passages of Calvin have been quoted by some (notably Emile Doumergue) as implying that Calvin did not hold to inerrancy. This evidence boomerangs, as was well shown by John K. Mickelsen, "The Relationship Between the Commentaries of John Calvin and His *Institutes of the Christian Religion*, and the Bearing of that Relationship on the Study of Calvin's Doctrine of Scripture," *The Gordon Review* 5, no. 4 (Winter 1959), pp. 155–68.

pose of the writers. It doesn't seem unreasonable to expect that the small residue of problems that presently remain will similarly be solved by an increase in the knowledge of Bible times. As it is, God has shed enough light on His Word so that we may recognize it as undoubtedly the Word of God; and He has permitted sufficient difficulties to remain so that those who wish to close their eyes may seem to have some reason for doing so.[17]

In some respects the sinlessness of our Lord Jesus Christ presents an analogous situation. The reality of His deity completely precludes the possibility that He should commit any sin, and the Scripture bears witness to the fact that He remained sinless throughout His days (John 8:46; 14:30; II Cor. 5:21; Heb. 4:15; 9:14; I Peter 2:22; I John 3:5). Now, there are some actions which He did or words that He uttered which in the life or on the lips of any other person might be deemed questionable. Our assurance of the sinlessness of Christ inevitably leads us to interpret these incidents in keeping with His deity, or else serious heresies will follow. Meanwhile, we do not go about fretting in the fear that some sin in the person of Christ might be discovered, but we maintain with confidence the sinlessness of our Lord in the assurance that the data will ultimately support our faith. The same principle applies to our attitude toward Scripture: Even though we may not at present see the complete harmony at every point, we trust that such harmony does exist and that it will in due course be made manifest by God Himself.

Inerrancy and Evangelical Truth

Some strong advocates of inerrancy have occasionally expressed themselves as if this doctrine were the necessary

---

17. Cf. Blaise Pascal, *Pensées,* no. 736 (Brunschvicq, no. 564) (London: Harvil Press, 1962), p. 332.

and sufficient standard of evangelical truth. Important as this tenet is, we should say here that it is not strictly either sufficient or necessary.

It is not sufficient because there are many other tenets that need to be maintained if a person is to be seen as clearly evangelical. Some who have turned to cults still adhere to the inerrancy of Scripture.[18] Thus, while the Evangelical Theological Society has made its confession of faith to pivot in this area,[19] this is not to say that no other doctrine matters. Meanwhile, our Roman Catholic friends who do use the word *inerrant* a good deal and have it incorporated in certain official statements[20] seem to have shown at times considerable laxity in the critical approach toward the Scripture.[21] The restrictions on the concept of inerrancy presently in vogue in many circles of the Roman Catholic Church are not reassuring. Thus, no one should imagine that the use of the word *inerrant* is an infallible preservative against any loosening of the faith. It is indeed a link in the chain but it does not constitute the whole chain.

On the other hand, inerrancy is not strictly a necessary tenet of evangelical truth. Some people who assert a limited errancy remain in other respects very solidly aligned with the evangelical movement. Here the much cited case

---

18. E.g., Jehovah's Witnesses and the Mormons, to name only two groups by their popular designation.

19. "The Bible alone, and the Bible in its entirety, is the Word of God written, and therefore inerrant in the autographs."

20. Leo XIII, Encyclical *Providentissimus Deus,* 18 November 1893, Denz 1952–53 (3292–93); Benedictus XV, Encyclical *Spiritus Paraclitus,* 15 September 1920, Denz 2186 (3652); Pius XII, Encyclical *Divino Afflante Spiritu,* 30 September 1943, Denz 2294 (3830); "Dogmatic Constitution on Divine Revelation," #11, in *The Documents of Vatican II,* ed. W. M. Abbott (New York: Guild Press, 1966), p. 119.

21. Jean Levie, *The Bible, Word of God in Words of Men* (New York: P. J. Kenedy & Sons, 1962), pp. 214–46; J. T. Burtchaell, *Catholic Theories of Biblical Inspiration Since 1810* (Cambridge: Cambridge University Press, 1969); Hans Küng, *Infallible? An Inquiry* (Garden City, NY: Doubleday, 1971), pp. 209–21.

of James Orr might be advanced. He did not rule out the possibility of errors of detail, but he averred that he never found anything in Scripture which would compel him to say that the Bible was wrong.[22] It would seem unfortunate to frame a definition of evangelical faith that would oblige us to deny the title of membership to a man like James Orr. Warfield himself, who surely showed no hesitancy in his advocacy of inerrancy, was ready to recognize in Orr a man of faith with whom he was pleased to collaborate.

What is supremely at stake in this whole discussion is the recognition of the authority of God in the sacred oracles. Are we going to submit unconditionally to the voice of God who has spoken? Or, are we going to insist on screening the message of the Bible, accepting only what appears palatable and remaining free to reject what does not conform to our preconceived criteria? This is really the great divide, and those who stress inerrancy are simply aiming to maintain what they view as the consistent biblical stance on this issue.

At the close of the Chicago Statement on Biblical Inerrancy this point is admirably expressed:

> In our affirmation of the authority of Scripture as involving its total truth, we are consciously standing with Christ and his apostles, indeed with the whole Bible and with the main stream of church history from the first days until very recently. We are concerned at the casual, inadvertent and seemingly thoughtless way in which a belief of such far-reaching importance has been given up by so many in our day.
>
> We are conscious too that great and grave confusion results from ceasing to maintain the total truth of the Bible

22. Orr wrote: "'Inerrancy' can never be demonstrated with a cogency which entitles it to rank as the foundation of a belief in inspiration" (*Revelation and Inspiration* [London: Duckworth, 1910], p. 199). Yet he also wrote a few pages later: "The Bible, impartially interpreted and judged, is free from demonstrable error in its statements, and harmonious in its teachings, to a degree that of itself creates an irresistible impression of a supernatural factor in its origin" (p. 216).

> whose authority one professes to acknowledge. The result of taking this step is that the Bible which God gave loses its authority, and what has authority instead is a Bible reduced in content according to the demands of one's critical reasonings and in principle reducible still further once this has started. This means that at bottom independent reason now has authority as opposed to scriptural teaching. If this is not seen and if for the time being basic evangelical doctrines are still held, persons denying the full truth of Scripture may claim an evangelical identity while methodologically they have moved away from the evangelical principle of knowledge to an unstable subjectivism, and will be hard put not to move further.[23]

The confession of biblical inerrancy, in the biblical sense of that concept, is simply one emphatic way to assert that what Scripture says, God says. To Him be the glory and the authority. Amen.

---

23. "Chicago Statement on Biblical Inerrancy," pp. 10–11. Printed, e.g., in Carl F. H. Henry, *God, Revelation and Authority* (Waco, TX: Word Books, 1979), vol. 4, p. 219.

DOUGLAS STUART

4

Inerrancy and Textual Criticism

Introduction to the Problem

The goal of textual criticism is to establish as far as is possible the original wording of the books of the Bible. Using fairly well-defined procedures, the textual critic collates copies of scriptural portions, whose exact wordings usually differ at certain points, in order to decide which wording is most likely that of the text when it was first written down.

On the surface, this would seem reasonable and proper enough. But Christians have frequently adopted two troublesome views toward the practice of textual criticism: they have concluded either that it is irrelevant and therefore unnecessary to the study of the Bible; or that it is a dangerous practice, threatening the concepts of the inspiration and accuracy of the Bible. Our purpose in this essay is to show that both of these views toward textual criticism are faulty and should be discarded in favor of the view that textual criticism, properly done, is both necessary to biblical scholarship, and a practical asset to the Bible student as well.

A word concerning the limits of textual difficulties in the Bible is in order. On the negative side, the problems are real. There is no chapter of the Bible for which all ancient manuscripts have exactly the same wording. Many chapters, in fact, display textual problems in virtually every verse. On the positive side, the problems are not overwhelming. The vast majority of textual divergencies involve an inability to choose between equally plausible and usually synonymous wordings, simple haplographies (losses of words) that do not affect the overall meaning of a passage, or conflations (adding words from elsewhere in the same book) which are often quite helpful to the sense of the passage.

Thus it would not be correct to suggest that the various ancient versions of the Bible are in hopeless disagreement with one another, or that the percentage of textual corruptions is so high as to render questionable large blocks of Scripture. Rather, it is fair to say that the verses, chapters, and books of the Bible would read largely the same, and would leave the same impression with the reader, even if one adopted virtually every possible *alternative* reading to those now serving as the basis for current English translations. In fact, absolutely nothing essential to the major doctrines of the Bible would be affected by any responsible decision in the area of textual criticism. Certain of the individual passages supporting a given doctrine might be subject to different interpretation if a different text were postulated, but in no case would all the passages relevant to a given doctrine be transformed in meaning by decisions about the wording of the texts.

A comparison of sample verses from several popular modern English versions of the Bible will give any reader a general idea of what the range of differences between texts might be—the modern English translations are themselves texts, and they roughly parallel the ancient version in the kinds and varieties of divergencies that are possible under normal circumstances.

Another way to gain a perspective on the nature of textual "corruptions" is to read through a daily newspaper. Most papers have a fairly high error rate, yet one can easily enough comprehend stories with minor typographical errors in them. Only when a story becomes totally garbled—fairly rare—is part of the meaning of the text actually lost to the reader.

Interestingly, textual criticism is a somewhat more complex task in the case of the Old Testament than in the New. This is because all the ancient Hebrew texts, unlike the Greek, were originally written without vowels. Moreover, the Old Testament texts, being older, were subject to many more years of copying and recopying, and were translated into other languages earlier in history than were the New Testament texts. A preponderance of our examples of textual problems will accordingly be chosen from the Old Testament.

The Original Autographs

An orthodox appreciation for the accuracy of the Bible is expressed in a variety of ways in various creeds and doctrinal statements. Evangelicals have often made use of a qualifying phrase when speaking of the fact that the Bible is without error, or entirely trustworthy. This qualifying phrase is usually something like: "in the original autographs." Such a qualification recognizes that there is no single copy or translation of the Bible that has universal acceptance and confidence. Regardless of denominational or confessional tradition, one is not likely to find any text of the Bible or portion thereof, whether ancient or modern, upon which there is formal agreement that it is faultless and absolutely reliable. For example, we would search in vain to find agreement among any major group of orthodox Christians that a given translation such as the Revised Standard Version is itself either "without error" or "entirely trustworthy."

Going back to the ancient texts themselves does not automatically solve the problem. We are all aware that in ancient times, without the precision of the printing press and other modern duplication aids, there were constant opportunities for minor and sometimes major differences in wordings of a given text to develop over a period of years. Consider the many hundreds of copies of parts or the whole of the Greek New Testament we have from ancient times. These represent, undoubtedly, just a small fraction of the vast number of copies that we may infer to have been in existence in the first few centuries after the death and resurrection of Jesus. Some of the copies we have may be only once or twice removed from the originals. But others are copies of copies, many times removed. Thus there are no two lengthy texts preserved from the early centuries that are exactly alike. It is impossible, in fact, to prove from the copies still in existence that there were ever any two that were precisely the same. The same situation applies in the Hebrew Old Testament texts, from which examples appear below.

The Fact of Divergencies

Why the differences? Why do we find variant readings on virtually every page when we turn from one manuscript to another? The answer lies in the fact that in ancient times people had to copy documents by hand. The hand is controlled by the brain, and the brain is not normally capable of the kind of precision required to produce exact, mirror images of long documents, except at very great sacrifice. Unless a person were willing to give the better part of a lifetime to laboriously checking and rechecking a copy of the Bible he had made, he would not be able to eliminate completely the divergencies in his own copy from the original text which he had copied. But ancient copyists had no such sacrifice in view. In the option between production and perfection, they wisely chose production. Their primary interest was to produce reasonably accurate copies which could then be passed on to persons eager to read the Word of God and to benefit from its truth. Such things as the differences in wordings between two copies of the same book of the Bible among the Dead Sea Scrolls, or the various marginal corrections and erasures in many ancient Greek and Hebrew texts, or the various later retranslations and corrections of the Hebrew and Greek Bibles still preserved from ancient times all confirm that there were multitudes of good *but not perfect* copies of the Bible in circulation in the old world. In fact, until well into the Middle Ages, there is little evidence of widespread concern for total precision of the sort that demands years of checking and rechecking a given manuscript for its accuracy. The first known development of an exhaustive attempt at textual precision in the case of the Old Testament, for example, occurred among a Jewish scholarly group called the Masoretes around the sixth century A.D. But the Old Testament had already been compiled, copied hundreds of times, translated and retranslated into several other languages long before the time of the Masoretes. This inevitably resulted in a considerable diversity of textual readings and divergent wordings in individual verses, chapters, and books within each of the language families of the translations, and among them all.

We can therefore see the wisdom of speaking about the inerrancy of the Bible in terms of "the original autographs" or "as originally given," so that the Bible is said to be inerrant or entirely trustworthy not in the copies or the translations, but in the original writing. Such a qualification is a sensible recognition of the fact that we modern Christians do not have a single copy of any book of the Bible exactly as it may have originally been written by the human author under the inspiration of the Holy Spirit. In fact, if we did happen to have an actual original wording, we would have no way to recognize it, since there are so many ancient versions of every book of the Bible, no two of which agree precisely as to all wordings. There is no pure copy to which all other texts may be compared.

We must therefore speak of the original autographs (from the hand of the authors) as theoretical entities only. It must be recognized that there have been "corruptions" of the original wording of virtually every substantial section of the Bible. The term *corruption* implies nothing more than that in a given text there have been some changes from the wording of the autograph. It is hardly possible, of course, to decide in every case what is a corruption and what is not. When two texts disagree, it is often difficult or even impossible to make a decision as to which of the two might in fact more closely represent the original autograph.

For this reason, an entire branch of biblical scholarship called textual criticism, or "lower" criticism,[1] has developed in order to give careful attention to such matters by utilizing procedures which can help approximate the autographs. The goal of textual criticism is to provide the best possible information about the original reading at a given point in the Scriptures.

The task is not an easy one. The effort to arrive at an original reading involves substantial effort, including the examination of large numbers of copies of any ancient text, often in several languages; careful analytical linguistic work using detailed philological methods; and extensive vocabulary and word-frequency analyses, among other techniques.

The following describes how a competent textual critic would approach the task of establishing (approximating the original of) the text of I Samuel 20, as in example (3) below.

---

1. So-called to distinguish it from "higher" criticism, which deals with matters of authorship, historical background, religious orientation, etc.

First, one would carefully compare the wordings and spellings of the medieval Masoretic Hebrew text with those in other Hebrew texts including the Dead Sea Scroll copy of Samuel, as well as the ancient Greek, Latin, Aramaic, and Syriac translations. After collecting all significant differences (several dozen) one would then analyze them group by group to attempt to decide whether the differences at a given point in the story can be explained by postulating a progression of copyists' errors, changes, or translation decisions. In the process one would start with the Hebrew and move through the different families of texts within the various language groups. In this complicated task, one would be guided by the results of other scholars' researches on the general tendencies toward changes in the type of text being examined, as documented from the books of Samuel as a whole. After perhaps weeks of full-time study, one might then be able to present some findings, including the *most likely* wordings of the original prior to the variety of changes which one believes took place subsequently and which he believes he can identify in a sequence of stages. Obviously, this substantial effort is still no guarantee of perfection. In fact, especially in the case of the Old Testament, there is not much hope that biblical scholarship can do more than chip away at the great iceberg of textual problems. That is, we have no surety that in the next hundred years even half of the major significant difficulties with the Old Testament text will be solved to general satisfaction. This is a discouraging fact which has led some people to seek one of two easy ways out.

Easy Solutions

The first path taken by many is simply to say that since no one text can be proved fully authoritative as opposed to any others, and since the establishment of an eclectic text is an elaborate process, we ought simply to flip a coin as it were and settle upon a single text by arbitrarily designating it as reliable. The problem with this method is that it ignores the principle that there is a greater chance for arriving at precision by examining many witnesses than by examining only one witness. Consider, for example, the textual problems inherent in the beginning of Romans 8:28, a verse often used to encourage believers who are enduring discouragement. There are three possible translations for this verse, depending on which Greek text one decides to use as the basis of his translation. The possible readings are: (1) "We know that all things work together for good to those who love God. . . "; (2) "We know that in everything he works for good to those who love him. . . "; (3) "We know that in all things God works for the good of those who love him. . . ."

Nearly all New Testament textual critics would agree that reading (3) is most likely the wording of the original, since it comes from a family of texts which in this particular case seems to have the greatest credibility and overall clarity of expression. Of course, the Bible student who arbitrarily chooses a text containing reading (1) would not even have the option of arriving at translation (3). He or she would possibly therefore continue to give currency to the notion that all bad events are blessings in disguise, even though it is most likely that the original words of Paul imply no such thing.

Likewise in the case of the Old Testament, we will probably get a clearer picture of the original if we examine several copies in ancient Hebrew, Greek, and other languages than if we arbitrarily pick out one of those several copies. After all, we might unwittingly choose the most damaged and altered text among the several—and then where are we? Picking one text arbitrarily is thus a very risky procedure indeed, one which rules out from the start any access to the valuable information that other texts of the same book could easily provide. In the long run the single-text approach is more subjective than the results of virtually any approach which takes the various versions into consideration. The fact that all modern New Testament translations are based upon an eclectic text rather than a single source, even though there are extant many ancient Greek New Testament texts from times much closer to the original date of composition than in the case of the Old Testament, should be evidence enough that good scholars do not consider a single text to be enough.

The second easy way out is to regard the whole textual critical process as somehow beneath the Christian and to presume on faith that the copies of the Bible that *we* have in English are divinely transmitted without errors having been allowed to creep in. We might call this the "golden plate" approach, because it hopes for a kind of miraculous accuracy in the process of copying and translating the Bible that simply cannot be supported historically.

In most cases, those who take this path are persons who either do not know or regularly work in the original biblical languages, or who have never had the opportunity to examine the known history of texts and versions. In some cases, however, a kind of de facto canonization of a single translation may take place in the mind of a Bible student who is in fact trained in the rudiments of textual criticism and who believes in principle that no single version is ultimately authoritative. By reason of a busy schedule and the general press of time, many pastors, for example, tend to fall into a pattern of reliance upon their favorite English translation of the Bible for even the most minute, detailed interpretative analysis of a passage.

Because the New Testament translations are based on an eclectic text, the pastor is usually in no danger of reading doctrinal heresy into a passage. But sometimes, such as in the case of Romans 8:28 illustrated above, he or she may unwittingly choose a reading that leads to a different inference about the message of the passage than the inspired author intended.

Since there is no single ancient Bible text that does not contain copyists' errors, gaps, garbled words, and other corruptions, the intelligent, reverent application of the principles of textual criticism in whatever measure possible is not just a luxury for the Bible student, but, ultimately, a necessity. To avoid the whole problem either by blind reliance upon a single textual tradition or by wishing perfection upon a given translation is not a helpful long-range solution. At their worst, these approaches encourage Christians to accept texts which have in them nonsense, gaps, and glosses (additions to the text), thus suggesting that the Holy Spirit was sometimes an inspirer of inferior material. Such approaches could in one sense be considered an insult to the Holy Spirit. They cannot conscientiously be adopted by the orthodox Christian.

Some Examples of Problems in Old Testament Textual Criticism

A few examples of the kinds of divergencies that exist among ancient manuscripts should help clarify the issues facing us in regard to the need for responsible textual criticism.

1. The Versions of Jeremiah

In most English Bibles the text of Jeremiah is translated from a Hebrew version referred to above as the Masoretic text. This text represents only one ancient (actually medieval) tradition of the wording of Jeremiah. The Septuagint, the Greek Old Testament, contains a text of Jeremiah which has approximately 12 percent fewer words than the text found in the standard Masoretic Old Testament. At one time it was assumed that the Septuagint had simply eliminated about an eighth of the material, for tendentious reasons. With the discovery of the Dead Sea Scrolls, however, the validity of the Greek shorter version was confirmed by a new text now called 4Q Jeremiah B. This is an ancient copy of the Hebrew Book of Jeremiah which is also one-eighth shorter than the Masoretic version. And in addition, there was found in the same Dead Sea cave a text now called 4Q Jeremiah A, which is not shorter, but about the same length as the Masoretic version! What does all this mean? For one thing, it is rather clear evidence (although by no means the only evidence) that in the ancient world there were in existence, side by side and held in reverence by the same pious preservers of the Bible texts, differing versions of Bible portions. The so-called *Kethib-Qere* discrepancies[2] of the Masoretic Hebrew Bible are also indications of the tendency of the ancients to live with more than one text form at a time. The modern Bible student who routinely consults more than one translation stands in this tradition.

With regard to the particular case of the versions of Jeremiah, the differences are not nearly as great as the discrepancy in length might seem to indicate. Fortunately, most of the variations are due to extensive repetitions in the standard Masoretic text (paralleled by 4Q Jeremiah A). It contains very little which is truly different from the Greek version as paralleled by 4Q Jeremiah B. Scholars call the lengthier version a "conflate" text. The issues of incompatibility or contradiction are really secondary. What the existence of these two versions of Jeremiah does demonstrate is how ancient copyists tended to make what they felt to be appropriate adjustments in the texts they received. Certain ancient copyists apparently felt free to conflate or assemble together various bits of a biblical book, adding from elsewhere in a book material that they

2. These are the hundreds of instances where the Masoretes retained the consonants of one textual tradition and the vowels of another in the same word. The consonants which were "written" (*Kethib*) in the authoritative text were not the consonants which were read (*Qere*).

thought relevant to a given chapter or passage. In most cases, such editorial work is welcome and helpful to the reader. We have no reason to fear it. It is in no way a threat to our confidence in the accuracy of God's revelation, but it does lead us to be cautious in judging what would constitute the original autograph in such cases.

The implications for our understanding of God's inspiration and preservation of the text cannot be ignored. Basically summarized, they are: (a) the integrity of the original revelation of God to an individual or group, resulting in the recording of what is now a portion of the Bible, is not in any way challenged by the practice of textual criticism; (b) the subsequent transmission of these writings, in some cases involving manifold stages, has produced by the nature of the imperfect transmissive media imperfect copies; (c) the inability to recover the original wordings easily or with complete certainty means that we must always maintain a degree of humility about our absolute knowledge of the original in any particular case; (d) upon close examination, it is clear that textual divergences and corruptions are never so massive or systematic that any doctrine which is in any sense broadly based (as are all significant Christian doctrines) could be considered threatened by the results of textual criticism.

2. I Samuel 21:4

In the story of the visit of David and his outlaw band to the sanctuary at Nob, the Masoretic text records the chief priest's remark to David: "I have no regular bread, but there is holy bread, if the men have abstained from women." The Septuagint, an equally reliable Old Testament copy, is joined by a text from the Dead Sea Scrolls (4Q Samuel B) in dividing the remark into two sentences, the second being more complete: "If the men have abstained from women, you may eat some of that."

In the Masoretic version we have an example of what is

called haplography. This means that something has been left out. The fuller text as recorded in the Septuagint and the Dead Sea Scrolls gives us a bit more detail in the story. Certainly we could not say that the Masoretic text is horribly defective or misleading—not at all. There is, nevertheless, a genuine difference in the Masoretic text from the other texts because a small amount of material has apparently dropped out in the course of transmission. What was left was an incomplete clause which was then construed to be the ending of the previous sentence rather than an independent sentence in itself. If one were attempting to reconstruct an original autograph, one would almost certainly conclude that the longer version, as recorded in the Septuagint and its Dead Sea Scroll parallel, would more likely preserve the original. This would be a recognition of the fact that the Masoretic text is just one ancient version, not sufficient in itself to allow us to reconstruct the original autographs. We need to compare *all* the relevant texts if we are to hope to approximate the wording of the inspired original.

3. I Samuel 20:34

In the story of Jonathan and David, the Masoretic text says in verse 34 of I Samuel 20: "Jonathan rose from the table." The Septuagint and 4Q Samuel B record, however: "Jonathan sprang up from the table." That is, the Septuagint and 4Q Samuel B employ a different verb from that which is employed by the Masoretic text. This illustrates what is known as replacement. In such cases, the Masoretic text has replaced the more difficult, more complicated verb, "sprang up," with a much simpler verb, "rose." At some point in the history of the transmission of the text, some copyist probably reasoned that people usually rise from tables rather than spring up from tables, and felt obliged to simplify or clarify the reading. Naturally, one could hardly conclude that there is a doctrinal difference at stake between the two readings, or that anything affecting our lives as Christians could be inferred from the differences in the readings. Rather, this example is a minor illustration of the usefulness of a principle commonly known in textual criticism as *lectio difficilior.* This principle says that in the long history of copying and recopying a text, there is a natural tendency for a scribe to replace a more difficult reading with a simpler one. Sometimes several ancient manuscripts can be arranged in chronological order and compared to see when such a change was made. When this is done, one often finds that the original reading was the rarer, more complicated word, with the simpler word being the replacement, since copyists tended to write down what was clear to them and to eliminate what was not, regardless of how they may have revered the text from which they were copying.[3] Therefore, we conclude that in the Masoretic text of I Samuel 20:34 we have a wording that is not original but that the wording in the Septuagint and the Dead Sea Scrolls is. Our English Old Testaments have traditionally followed the Masoretic text at this point, and therefore are also not as truly faithful to the original as they could be. Why? It is not because translators do not desire to be faithful to the original—but because thorough textual analysis is so time-consuming that translators can rarely afford to indulge in it if they wish to complete their translations in their own lifetimes.

Some Inferences

Some people may feel that textual criticism will expose weaknesses in the ancient versions of the Bible or the translations made from them. This is not really the case.

---

3. For a number of reasons, including the vowelless Hebrew orthography of the early periods, *lectio difficilior* is not as reliable in Old Testament textual analysis as it is in New Testament textual analysis.

What textual criticism shows is that no single version can claim to be perfect, since there are evident differences in the ancient copies. In this sense, strength comes with diversity. Since we have available to us a great variety of ancient texts, we must whenever possible place them before us and analyze them. The results will give us a far greater security as to what the original may have been than the credulous certification of any one text could ever do. We are therefore obliged not to reject whatever complicates the picture, but to enter into a careful and responsible analysis of the texts we have in an attempt to decide what was most likely the original wording actually inspired by the Holy Spirit.

Interestingly, in the case of some books we cannot rule out the possibility that a single original autograph as such never really existed. Consider the Book of Psalms, for example. It is widely agreed that the psalms in the Old Testament were composed at various times, in a variety of places, by a variety of authors. The psalms themselves indicate this. They were finally put together at some point into the current book of 150 that we now have. It would be absurd to suggest that all 150 psalms were written at once in the order in which we now have them. That would assume, for example, that Moses was contemporaneous with David, since both Moses and David authored psalms that are now included in the current 150. No, we must recognize that the Book of Psalms is a compilation of various original autographs. As a result, we must speak in terms of stages of composition and collection, rather than a single time of writing. The psalm of Moses, Psalm 90, had at first its own history, as well as the history it had as part of the Book of Psalms after all 150 were grouped together. What then is the original autograph of the Book of Psalms? Perhaps there is not an original autograph as such. One might better speak first of an original autograph of a given psalm, then an original autograph of whatever intermediate collections of psalms may have existed (some of which are mentioned in the superscriptions), and then finally the autograph of the entire book with which we currently deal. Thus the concept of autograph can be somewhat fluid and must be adapted to meet the criteria involved in a given biblical book. None of this is in any sense incompatible with traditional, orthodox doctrines of revelation and inspiration. The Scripture's own witness to the process of inspiration recognizes the potential for diversities therein: "In the past God spoke to our forefathers through the prophets *at many times and in various ways* . . . " (Heb. 1:1, NIV). Inspiration is a process—the time necessary for the process to have taken place, or the number of stages in the process itself may have varied from case to case. The final result is still an inspired, trustworthy Scripture, though not necessarily a single pristine copy thereof.

The Evangelical Outlook Toward Textual Criticism

For the evangelical, the original text of a portion of Scripture is of real interest. Of course, we must keep in consideration that the final form a lengthy portion of Scripture assumes may seem quite different from the form of the individual subunits. By the mere force of its consistency, completeness, and applicability, the final piecing together may be more important and is likely to be more authoritative than the subunits in scattered isolation. At any rate, we are all eager to relate ourselves to the original Word of God in a form as free as possible from whatever accretions or distortions may have affected it during the long history of its transmission to our present day.

Because this is precisely the goal of textual criticism—the arrival at the coherent original—textual criticism must in fact be seen as supportive of the evangelical enterprise. An evangelical who does biblical scholarship at a high level will necessarily involve himself in textual criticism since he desires to interpret and apply the Word of God as it was originally given, not as it has been encumbered by transmissive or translational difficulties, be they major as in a few cases, or minor, as in the vast majority of cases.

Three Categories of Discrepancies

Upon careful investigation, one finds that the most blatant discrepancies that exist in the extant texts, such as the so-called contradictions in the Bible, most often involve one of three simple categories: names, dates, and numbers. It is these three areas that throughout the history of literature have been most easily subject to distortion and corruption in copying. They are by their very nature variable features which cannot be determined from the context. By this we mean that specific names, dates, and numbers are items which cannot be grammatically predicted in a sentence, or be remembered by reason of the word order or the general meaning. For example, consider the following two sentences that might be recorded as spoken by a town official of some sort at a time in the past: "Joe was our police chief at the time of the great fire"; and "John was our police chief at the time of the great fire." Since we do not personally know either Joe or John, and it seems reasonable that there was only one chief of police in the town at the time of the great fire, we simply have no way of knowing whether it was Joe or John. That is, nothing in the names themselves can tell us which one was the police chief. Names can vary freely. Any one of thousands of names could have been used in that sentence. Maybe both Joe and John served as police chief in succession, but we do not know that. It would be relatively easy therefore for a copyist to get the name wrong.

A copyist would not, however, have been likely to write these sentences: "Joe was our homecoming queen at the time of the great fire"; or "John was our homecoming queen at the time of the great fire." The reason such sentences would not likely be written is that the copyist would realize that they are illogical, would stop to check what he or she was copying, and would keep from writing such nonsense. It is a general rule, therefore, that the more meaningful portions of sentences do not as easily become corrupted as do those words which are without particular meaning to a copyist in a given context.

The same situation is true of dates as well as numbers. Consider the following example: "Harold the Great died in 1046." If you were a scribe copying this sentence from an ancient document, and you did not otherwise know when Harold the Great died, you might accidentally write in your own copy, "Harold the Great died in 1064," or "Harold the Great died in 1604." The date means little to you, and there is nothing in the context to tell you whether any particular date is right or wrong. It becomes relatively easy for you to make a mistake under those circumstances. The same principle obviously applies to numbers as well.

There are many biblical passages where problems arise as a result of faulty transmission of names, dates, or numbers. For example, the disputed identification of Quirinius as governor of Syria in Luke 2:2 might conceivably be due to just such a problem of names—either in the history of transmission of the texts of the Book of Luke, or the texts of other ancient historical records which do not seem to correspond to Luke 2:2 in this regard.

Again, in II Kings 17:4 it is reported that the Israelite King Hoshea "sent messengers to So, king of Egypt." As far as all ancient Egyptian records indicate, there never was a king named So. Thus, many scholars have speculated that either the name *So,* or the title *king of Egypt,* in some way has been disturbed in the long history of the transmission of the text.

Problems associated with the precise dates of the reigns of some Israelite kings (such as King Pekah), with the identification of certain Israelite priests (such as Ahimelech), or with names of sites (such as Ai) have all at one time or another been cited to suggest that the Bible record is in some way unsatisfactory. Such an accusation is very wide of the mark. Compared to most other ancient historical documents of significant length, the Bible contains relatively few questions about names, dates, and numbers.

As a result, the recognized difficulties in both the New and the Old Testaments with regard to names, dates, and numbers should not be of great concern to those with a deep respect for the accuracy of the Scripture. It is simply the case that in these categories we are going to find a larger number of transmissive corruptions than we will find in any other categories. When we come to significant doctrinal matters, however, matters affecting outlook and practice, few accusations against the ancient texts themselves are heard. The demonstrable problems tend to be found in the more insignificant areas of technical historical details, rather than in the important areas of faith, morals, and application for our lives. These important areas do not depend upon variable elements such as names, dates, or numbers, and thus are not likely to contain the types of textual difficulties which would affect their overall meaning.

Textual criticism is valuable. It heads us in the direction of the original. It is not to be feared, but is friend rather than foe. Certainly the practice of textual criticism does involve personal judgments, frequent uncertainties, and a willingness on the part of the textual critic to admit that he or she does not often know the answer to a given problem. There is no guarantee that the original reading of the text will always be recoverable. But the results on the whole are quite encouraging. For example, it has been argued that 99 percent of the original words in the New Testament are recoverable with a very high degree of certainty. In the case of the Old Testament, the figure might be more like 95 percent. When the words that are recoverable with a fairly high degree of certainty are added, we may be confident that we are able to read, reflect upon, and act upon what is practically equivalent to the original itself. There is no area of Christian faith or practice that actually stands or falls on the basis of textual studies.

The Practical Benefits of Textual Criticism

Textual criticism can actually be of help to us in several ways. First, it can keep us from an overemphasis upon a single word or verse in the Bible. That is, where there is a healthy respect for the possibility that the text in its received state may be subject to improvement, we will tend not to place undue stress upon a single word for a major doctrinal point. Basic doctrine should depend as much as possible upon widely represented teachings of the Scripture, and not upon a problematic wording in a single verse. A doctrine should reflect faithfully the clear message of the Scripture, as it is fully expressed, rather than a single debatable occasion where the choice of one reading over another is the basis for advancing the doctrine. The recognition of both the results and the difficulties of textual criticism should therefore help make evangelical Christians wise to the importance of the whole counsel of God, and tend to move them away from a practice for which they have been criticized for many years—"proof texting," the selective use of biblical statements out of context for biased ends.

The task is not an easy one. Evangelicals will always need to exercise caution regarding the results of radical textual criticism, the kind of textual analysis that goes far beyond basic "lower" (strictly textual) criticism to subjective, speculative emendation of texts to suit particular theological biases. This is not the kind of enterprise with which we are concerned in this essay. On the contrary, evangelicals can benefit from the recognition that they are not expected to try to defend a single set of texts currently used, to some extent arbitrarily, as the basis for many modern English translations as if these texts were pristine, perfect in every way. Evangelicals are free to admit weaknesses in the current copies of the Bible that are in their possession, while enthusiastically and confidently proclaiming the inerrancy or entire trustworthiness of the content of the faith once for all divinely delivered in the text of Scripture.

R. C. SPROUL

5

Biblical Interpretation and the Analogy of Faith

With the massive rupture of Christendom into a multitude of denominational fragments, the Reformation faced the crisis of finding a unified basis of authority. Though Protestant thinkers could agree that Scripture was to be the normative authority for the church (*Sola Scriptura*), they could not always agree on what that authority taught. Early in the Reformation the need for a sober and objective hermeneutic was clearly perceived. What emerged became known classically as the "Analogy of Faith."

Simply stated, the Analogy of Faith expressed the cardinal rule of biblical interpretation: "Scripture is to be its own interpreter." *Sacra Scriptura sui ipsius interpres.* This cardinal rule, which appears to be quite simple, is built on a host of complex assumptions that are not always immediately apparent.

The Assumptions or Presuppositions of the Analogy of Faith

1. The Scriptures are unified

At the heart of the Analogy of Faith is the clear conviction that the Scriptures do not manifest a chaotic smorgasbord of theological ideas. Though a wide diversity of styles, perspectives, and cultural settings is found in Scripture, the diversity is brought together by a unified theology. The traditional formula that the Bible is the words of men, yet the Word of God, attests to that assumption of unity. That theology could be thought to be "systematic" is further evidence.

This assumption of unity is no longer taken for granted in biblical scholarship. The widespread antipathy to systematic theology, the prevalence of atomistic exegesis, and the dominance of an underlying post-Kantian philosophy in biblical studies all call attention to the tenuous status of the Analogy of Faith in our day.

After Kant's disjunction between the "noumenal" world and the "phenomenal" world a crisis occurred with respect to basic approaches to knowledge. Kant's critique of natural theology carried with it a skeptical verdict about man's ability to achieve scientific knowledge of God, the self, and essences. Science was left with the realm of tangible objects and appearances (phenomena) as its area of investigation. Out of this schema emerged a complex of philosophical schools which restricted knowledge to the phenomenological realm (e.g., existentialism, positivism, and pragmatism).

The point of commonality for phenomenological approaches is found in their restricting knowledge to the *particulars* of the appearances of this world. No hope is given of discovering transcendent universals. Such universals are metaphysical and are thus said to be unknowable by ordinary means of knowledge.

How does this shift in philosophical method affect biblical exegesis? The process of restricting knowledge to particulars and eliminating universals confines knowledge to the level of diversity. *"Truths" can be known, but not truth.* Purposes can be discovered but not purpose. Values can be found but not value. We have diversity but no unity. The motto of this method is "*E pluribus plura.*" The atoms of knowledge can be analyzed but no essence can be formed from them. Atomistic exegesis gives close examination to particular passages of Scripture with no concern about relating them in a unified way with the whole of Scripture. If diversity in all of particulars is all we can know, unity is obscured. If unity is considered a priori unknowable, then there is no need to seek a unified view of truth. Atomistic exegesis is then not only permitted but demanded.

Though Kant believed in the reality of essences, the self, and God, he located them beyond the reach of ordinary ways of knowing. His theory of being (his ontology) allowed for God and unity, but his theory of knowing (his epistemology) left us with no objective way of reaching God. Some of his successors embraced his epistemological skepticism and rejected his ontological optimism. For them, diversity is all there is.

From Husserl to Käsemann, we see the gradual eclipse of a unified view of truth. Biblical scholars even within the evangelical tradition succumb daily to a phenomenological perspective without realizing it. One's *method* of biblical interpretation reveals one's underlying epistemology, which in turn reveals one's basic ontology. The tragedy of atomistic exegesis is that it declares implicitly an epistemology and consequently an ontology that are on a collision course with Christian theism.

It is the unity of Scripture that prompted the church to seek a systematic theology. There are two ways by which we can construct a systematic theology. The first is by bringing a preconceived system of truth or philosophy to the Scripture and forcing Scripture into conformity with it. The second way is to seek the inherent unity in the Scripture. This is precisely what the analytical method of epistemology is designed to do. The analytical method searches particulars in order to discover universals. It combines both induction and deduction.

So many examples of the former kind of "systematic theology" have been seen in church history that the term *systematic theology* has become anathema to many biblical scholars. A great danger of overreaction exists which may drive biblical scholars, innocently and unknowingly, right into the arms of a phenomenological atomism. Here the cure becomes more deadly than the disease.

The Analogy, however, provides a system on the basis of the Bible's own unity. That unity must account adequately for all biblical diversity. The whole can neglect none of its parts or the system is artificial. The conviction of the Analogy is that the sum of the parts will produce a unified whole.

2. The Scriptures are coherent

That the Scriptures are coherent follows by necessity from the assumption that they are unified. If the Scriptures are unified, they are also coherent and consistent. Diversity does not destroy coherence unless there is no transcendent unifying principle. If the Bible represented merely human opinions, over a vast number of centuries, on an equally vast number of issues, we could not realistically expect to find total coherence. But, if the Bible represents a unified Word of God, coherence is not only expected, but assured.

Evangelical efforts to harmonize difficult texts (particularly in the Synoptics) have been met with great ridicule. Accusations of Aristotelian paranoia and fundamentalistic naiveté have been frequent. The ridicule has been so persistent and loud that evangelicals have often been intimidated to the point of ceasing their efforts of harmonization and leaving it in the hands of higher critics. It is ironic that the best work of harmonization can now be found among the higher critics as they debate with each other over what is original and authentic and what is later interpolation.

Again, a phenomenological methodology is no more concerned with coherence in the Scriptures than it is with unity. It is better first to assume and then to seek inherent coherence. Without such an assumption, an objective hermeneutic is not only not possible, it is not desirable.

3. The Scriptures are rational

If the Scriptures are unified and coherent, then they are of a rational character. That is not to say they are a product of rational speculation or that they are structured in a syllogistic form. It is merely to say they are intelligible to the mind and do not violate the basic canons of logic. Coherence precludes contradiction. That which is contradictory is not coherent and is consequently unintelligible. Only when the principle of coherence is abandoned can men glory in contradictions. One cannot harmonize a contradiction. By the nature of the case, the contradiction manifests disharmony. The contradiction is the hallmark of incoherence.

A basic understanding of the principles of logic is necessary for sound exegesis. Fewer errors of exegesis are caused by ignorance of Greek grammar than by unwarrantable inferences drawn from the words themselves. The "laws of immediate inference" govern the legitimacy and validity of deductions drawn from the text. Exegesis becomes *eisegesis* when no rules of inference control the interpreter. How many times has the Pelagian notion of man's natural ability to respond to the gospel been argued from the text, "Whoever believes in him shall not perish" (John 3:16, NIV)? The text says nothing about who does believe or who can believe. It says that whoever does A (believes) will not do B (perish). A logical analysis of the words themselves will reveal the limits of implication.

The law of contradiction serves as an objective test of coherence. Simply stated the law says, "A cannot be A and non-A at the same time and in the same relationship." The pen I am using cannot be a pen and not a pen at the same time and in the same relationship. It can be a pen and a pointer at the same time, but this implies a difference in relationship. A passage of Scripture may have many applications and many nuances of meaning, but contrary nuances or applications are intolerable if the Scriptures are of a rational character.

Since rationalism in its various forms has been a traditional foe of biblical Christianity, some Christian scholars look askance at using principles of logic as tools for biblical interpretation. In this they often are confusing rationalism (which is an *ism*) with rationality, which only implies "being reasonable." Logic is seen as the invention of Aristotle and its use an unhealthy intrusion of pagan thought forms into the purity of faith. But Aristotle no more invented logic than Columbus invented America. Invention and discovery are not identical. What Aristotle did was simply to formulate principles that govern intelligible discourse. Even he recognized that logic is not a philosophy. Logic has no intrinsic content. It is, as Aristotle called it, the *organon* of all science. Logic is the instrument or tool by which reality can be understood.

Faith without reason is superstition. Faith against logic is irrationality. To use logic in biblical interpretation is to seek the Bible's inner coherence and unity. Logic serves as a governor to restrain us from whimsical and arbitrary interpretation.

It is of critical importance to understand three concepts if we are to avoid confusion concerning the rational character of Scripture. These are the concepts of contradiction, paradox, and mystery. Frequently, these three are confused and used as if they were synonyms. Variant accounts in the Gospels are sometimes called contradictions merely because they do not say the same thing or because they report different data. For example, are the Synoptic accounts of the resurrection contradictory because Luke mentions two angels at the tomb and Mark mentions only one? If Luke said there were two and Mark said there was *only* one, we would have a contradiction in the accounts. But, if there were in fact two, then by necessity there was also one. The accounts are indeed variant but not contradictory. Dealing with textual differences poses one kind of problem; dealing with contradictions poses quite another kind.

Loose talk about contradictions has not helped biblical scholarship. Contradictions are capable of being tested by formal standards. Venn Diagrams, for example, may be used to test alleged contradictions. Such diagrams applied to the Synoptic question of the number of angels at the tomb yield objective evidence that the accounts, though variant, are not contradictory.

The word *paradox* is being used more and more as a synonym for contradiction. Dialectical theology has been principally responsible for this confusion of terminology. Webster defines a paradox as "a statement that seems contradictory, unbelievable, or absurd but that may actually be true in fact." The key to the definition is found in the word *seems.* Etymologically, the term *paradox* derives from the Greek prefix *para* (alongside or beyond) and the verb *dokein* (to seem, to think). Classically, a paradox is an apparent contradiction which may be resolved under closer scrutiny.

Many statements sound contradictory at first hearing but under analysis reveal their unity. The problem of paradox (which Gordon Clark calls a "charley horse between the ears") can be seen in ecumenical confessional formulations of the Trinity and the person of Christ. The Chalcedonian formulation for Christ, that He is *vere homo* and *vere deus,* is a case in point. Recently, I heard a college professor of comparative religion assert that Christianity is irrational because it maintains (à la Chalcedon) that Jesus is 100 percent God and 100 percent man. Thus, if all of Jesus is God and all of Jesus is man, unless deity and humanity are essentially the same, Jesus is a contradiction and Christianity is irrational. However, Chalcedon did not say that all of Jesus is God and all of Jesus is man. It was precisely that irrational notion that Chalcedon condemned. Chalcedon said that Jesus is *truly* man and *truly* God with no mention of percentages. The formula *one* person and *two* natures does not violate the law of contradiction. It may be paradoxical in that the words appear (as they do to the professor in question) to be contradictory, but under formal analysis the contradiction yields.

The same problem occurs with the classic formula for the Trinity. Some see in it an exercise in irrational mathematics where $1 + 1 + 1 = 1$. Again, the formula—one in essence, three in person—is not contradictory. It can be broken down to read one in *A*, three in *B*. If we said the Trinity is one in essence and three in essence at the same time and in the same relationship, we would violate the canons of logic.

What the incarnation and the Trinity manifest are examples of profound mystery. A mystery is a truth that is beyond the scope and grasp of human reason. There is much about God that our finite minds cannot penetrate. The incomprehensibility of God is a basic article of Christian faith. But again, to labor the point, incomprehensibility is not irrationality. Because all that is irrational is incomprehensible does not mean that all that is incomprehensible is irrational.

That the Bible contains mystery should not offend us. If we encounter mysteries in our investigation of the finite world, how much more should we expect to encounter them in our quest for understanding the infinite! Who has penetrated the mysteries of light, gravity, motion, and energy? These foundational notions of modern science remain without precise ontological formulations. Functional or "economic" definitions abound, but their ontology remains obscure.

The assumption in the Analogy of Faith that Scripture is rational provides the practical rule of exegesis: no part of Scripture may be interpreted in such a way as to bring it into contradiction with another part of Scripture. Here is the Scripture-interprets-Scripture principle in action. For example, if we read in Scripture, "God is not willing that any should perish" (II Peter 3:9), how are we to interpret it? We know that the word *will* has several different possible meanings with respect to God. "Will" can refer to God's sovereign efficacious will by which God brings to pass whatever He decides. It can refer to His preceptive will by which He commands obedience. It can refer to His will of disposition, in terms of what pleases Him. These are but three of several possible interpretations.

The Analogy of Faith provides a broad context for interpretation that goes far beyond the immediate context of a verse. The Analogy puts clear limits on our preferences for assigning a particular meaning to a word. If we interpret the verse under consideration in terms of God's sovereign efficacious will, the meaning would be that no one ever perishes. If we think in terms of God's preceptive will, the meaning would be that no one is allowed or permitted to perish. If we think in terms of disposition, the meaning would be that God is not pleased with the perishing of the wicked. The first alternative brings the verse into sharp contradiction with everything else the Bible teaches about hell. The second makes no sense in light of the biblical teaching of the law. The third is quite compatible with what the rest of Scripture says concerning the disposition of God. The Analogy would demand the third alternative because the immediate context must rationally harmonize with the total context of Scripture.

Doesn't this procedure beg the question concerning the nature of Scripture, its inspiration and infallibility? In one sense, it does, if inspiration is arbitrarily assumed and contradictions are ruled out as impossible before any analysis of the texts of Scripture is made. In the past those who advocated the Analogy of Faith were, of course, committed to inspiration and that principle governed their hermeneutics—but not in an arbitrary way. We will explore the assumption of inspiration later.

But even without inspiration, the Analogy provides a valid method of interpreting any document. Common courtesy would demand that if an author's words were capable of two or more meanings, the burden of proof would be on those who insisted on the alternative that automatically brought the author into a state of self-contradiction. We are all quite capable of contradicting ourselves and, in fact, frequently do it. But no one appreciates such an accusation when he is innocent of self-contradiction. Thus, the Analogy provides the principle of the benefit of the doubt, if nothing else.

Furthermore, to outlaw contradictions on the basis of an arbitrary a priori assumption would be *petitio principii* (question-begging) of the worst sort. That is not the intent of the Analogy of Faith.

4. The Scriptures are capable of propositional analysis

The debate over *propositional revelation* that has gone on over the past few decades has left some thinking that the Bible is incapable of propositional analysis. For example, Bernard Zylstra writes:

> Historical relativism, however, is not the only source of undermining the authority of the Scriptures. In polar tension with it we find, especially in orthodox theological circles, a revival of rationalistic propositionalism. Here the Bible is looked upon as the Word of God because it contains "propositional truth." That is, *rational verbal statements that are true in and of themselves.* In this conception, the texts

> of the Bible are rational propositional statements. This view also undermines the authority of the Bible as God's Word, because the Bible does not contain "rational" verbal statements that are true in and of themselves.[1]

Zylstra expresses opposition to the argument that the Bible is the Word of God because it contains propositional truth. But no one really says that! Rather, it should be maintained that the Bible contains propositional truth because it is the Word of God. The truth is, of course, not "in and of itself," but it is propositional truth.

Zylstra says, "In this conception, the texts of the Bible are rational propositional statements." What is wrong with that? That the Bible is rational has already been discussed. That it contains statements needs no labored defense. That those statements are of a propositional character does need elucidation. Note Webster's definition of the word *proposition:* "in logic, an expression in which the predicate affirms or denies something about the subject."

Let us see if the Bible contains propositional statements:

> But now is Christ risen from the dead, and become the first fruits of them that slept. (I Cor. 15:20, KJV)

Here is a statement with a *subject* (Christ) and a compound *predicate* (is risen and become) in which two extraordinary affirmations are made. If that is not a propositional statement, what is it?

To be sure, the literary style of Scripture does not follow a format of mathematical or geometric theorems. Much of Scripture is poetic in form, but practically all the Bible is propositional in form. Being propositional, it is subject to the normal rules of grammar, syntax, and linguistic analysis.

---

1. Bernard Zylstra et al., *Will All the King's Men* (Toronto: Wedge Publishing Foundation, 1972), p. 183.

Luther recognized the propositional character of the Bible when he wrote:

> No "implication" or "figure" may be allowed to exist in any passage of Scripture unless such be required by some obvious feature of the words. . . . We should stick to just the simple, natural meaning of the words, as yielded by the rules of grammar and the habits of speech that God has created among men; for if anyone may devise "implication" and "figures" in Scripture at his own pleasure, what will all Scripture be but a reed shaken with the wind, and a sort of chameleon.[2]

Because biblical propositions are conveyed by a multitude of literary forms, the science of genre analysis is of great importance. A common-sense approach to Scripture demands that biblical texts be interpreted according to their literary genre. In propositional statements, verbs remain verbs and nouns remain nouns whether they are inspired by the Holy Ghost or uttered by barbarians.

Genre analysis is necessary for sober interpretation. To impose upon poetic structures categories of interpretation which apply to declarative statements is distortive. To impose poetic categories on declarative statements is also distortive.

At the point of genre analysis, we find much "weaseling" in biblical interpretation. Here is where the exegete must be scrupulous in his linguistic analysis to avoid turning the Bible into Luther's "chameleon." It is very easy to fall into the temptation of reinterpretation of biblical texts according to standards that are alien to the text itself. To force the Bible into categories of modern existentialism in order to make the Bible "relevant" is to commit literary vandalism. Bultmann's rejection of objectivity in favor of approaching the Bible with a "prior understanding" (*Vor-*

---

2. Martin Luther, *The Bondage of the Will,* trans. J. I. Packer and O. R. Johnston (Westwood, NJ: Fleming H. Revell, 1957), p. 192.

verständnis) drawn from Heidegger's ontology is an example of this.

Of course, there are times when literary analysis becomes very problematic. How does the verb "to be" function in Scripture? In some cases it serves as a copula; in others it is used in an obviously figurative way. Jesus' statement, "I am the door," is obviously figurative. His statement, "This is my body," is not so obvious. Luther's insistence on the declarative use of the verb "to be" in this statement made unification of the Lutheran and Reformed movements impossible in the sixteenth century.

Though literary analysis is not always a simple matter, it is a prerequisite for sober exegesis. Without it, the Bible becomes a waxed nose to be shaped according to the whim or prejudice of the reader.

5. The Bible is clear

A vital presupposition of the Analogy of Faith is the Reformation conviction of the perspicuity of Scripture. This conviction led to momentous historical repercussions, not the least of which was the controversial matter of translating the Bible into the vernacular, thus making it available to the laity.

The principle of perspicuity did not teach that all parts of the Bible are equally clear. It was recognized that some portions of Scripture are quite obscure and difficult to interpret. Rather, the principle called attention to two essential points of interpretation. The first is that *the basic message of the Bible is clear enough for the unskilled person to understand.* The message of salvation in Christ is not obscure. It was this point that motivated translations into the vernacular.

The second essential point which follows from the principle of perspicuity is that *what is obscure in one part of Scripture is often made clear in another part.* Hence, the Analogy of Faith functions as a tool of clarification. It is also a crucial restraint for tendencies of Gnostic interpretation. The practical rule of interpretation flowing out of perspicuity is that what is obscure in the Bible is to be interpreted by what is clear. The Gnostics, with their superior mystical insight, often interpreted the clear in light of the obscure in order to support their claims of superior knowledge. The violation of this second point of interpretation has resulted in a myriad of cultic distortions of Christianity.

The charge of neo-Gnosticism frequently leveled against Bultmann rests upon his principle of "prior understanding."[3] If a person must understand something like Heidegger's *Sein und Zeit* before he can "ask the right questions" of Scripture, then the Bible becomes a closed book except to the philosophical elite.

In addition to the points mentioned above, the Reformers also distinguished between internal and external perspicuity. This distinction calls attention to objective interpretation of the words of Scripture and subjective appropriation of them to the heart of the reader. There is an external, objective meaning to Scripture that can be understood by any interpreter, pagan or Christian. There is the internal significance of personal application and love that is not discovered apart from the work of the Holy Spirit. This is the "spiritual discernment" about which Scripture itself speaks.

The external-internal distinction protects two flanks. On the one hand it recognizes that there is some revelation which is not fully grasped apart from the Spirit's work of illumination. On the other hand it speaks against the idea that the Bible can be interpreted only by mystics. What the Bible says can be interpreted accurately without the Holy Ghost. The devil himself is capable of doing sound

---

3. Cf. Oscar Cullmann, *Salvation in History* (New York: Harper & Row, 1967), pp. 22–24.

exegesis. However, the saving power of God's Word will never penetrate the heart without the work of the Spirit. That the Bible can be interpreted objectively without subjective appropriation guards against "pneumatic" exegesis, by which any meaning can be attached to Scripture by a special appeal to private illumination granted by the Holy Ghost. The practical application of the distinction is twofold. On the one hand it calls us to a posture of prayer and dependency on the Holy Spirit for internal clarity; on the other hand it regards prayer as no substitute for linguistic analysis of the text. Luther put it this way:

> I certainly grant that many passages in the Scripture are obscure and hard to elucidate, but that is due, not to the exalted nature of their subjects, but to our own linguistic and grammatical ignorance; and it does not in any way prevent our knowing all the contents of Scripture. . . . If you speak of *internal* perspicuity, the truth is that nobody who has not the Spirit of God sees a jot of what is in the Scriptures. . . . If on the other hand, you speak of *external* perspicuity, the position is that nothing whatsoever is left obscure or ambiguous, but all that is in the Scripture is through the Word brought forth into the clearest light and proclaimed to the whole world.[4]

6. The Scriptures are inspired

The crisis of the biblical hermeneutics of this century is directly related to the confusion surrounding the question of the nature of Scripture. There is one sense in which the Analogy of Faith need not assume inspiration for its validity, but there is another sense in which this assumption is of crucial import.

In one sense the Analogy maintains that the Bible ought to be interpreted like any other book. This applies to matters of external perspicuity. That is, again, inspiration does

4. Luther, *Bondage of the Will,* pp. 70–74.

not change poetry into prose, or a verb into a noun. Word meanings are discovered by lexicology rather than prayer.

On the other hand the assumption of inspiration more than any other assumption not only lends itself to the Analogy of Faith but requires and demands the Analogy. If the Bible is inspired by God, then to set one part of it against another is to make God speak with a forked tongue. If the Bible is the word of man without inspiration, though courtesy may apply the Analogy to a point, there is no need to be overscrupulous about it or to apply it absolutely. Without inspiration the human words may be criticized and corrected by the interpreter. For example, Paul's "mistakes" may be corrected by twentieth-century theologians.

If the Bible is the inspired Word of God, no such corrections may be made; that is, unless God inspired mistakes of content. Here the truth of Scripture is at stake.

To be sure, the question of whether or not inspiration demands inerrancy as a logical corollary is a hotly disputed issue today. Those who maintain that inspiration demands inerrancy are criticized for imposing a foreign variety of Greek logic on Scripture. This criticism empties inspiration of content and slanders the Holy Ghost. The connection between inspiration, inerrancy, and the Analogy of Faith is not a matter of the "domino theory," but a matter of truth and consistency. Inspiration without inerrancy is an empty term. Inerrancy without inspiration is unthinkable. The two are inseparably related. They may be *distinguished* but not separated.

So it is with hermeneutics. We can easily distinguish between the inspiration and the interpretation of the Bible, but we cannot separate them. Anyone can confess a high view of the nature of Scripture but the ultimate test of one's view of Scripture is found in his method of interpreting it. A person's hermeneutic reveals his view of Scripture more clearly than does an exposition of his view.

The Analogy of Faith is indeed a weighty principle. It is

loaded with the presuppositions of (1) the unity of Scripture, (2) the coherence of revelation, (3) the rational character of God's Word, (4) the propositional character of Scripture, (5) the perspicuity of Scripture, and (6) the inspiration and inerrancy of Scripture.

JOHN JEFFERSON DAVIS

6

Genesis, Inerrancy, and the Antiquity of Man

The publication in 1859 of Charles Darwin's *Origin of Species* initiated a continuing debate in both Protestant and Catholic circles concerning how new scientific discoveries about human origins and the antiquity of the race could be reconciled with the early chapters of Genesis. The new discoveries in geology and anthropology seemed to pose serious challenges to the Christian doctrines of the *imago Dei,* original sin, and the inerrancy of Scripture. Thus the questions about the relationship between science and Scripture posed by the discoveries of Copernicus and Newton were intensified in the nineteenth century by the Darwinian theory of evolution. Do science and Scripture really conflict? Does the Bible *intend* to teach scientific truth? If so, in what sense? Would "incidental" scientific or historical errors be compatible with plenary inspiration? To what extent, if any, is strict scientific and historical accuracy in the modern sense of the term necessary in light of the central redemptive purpose of Scripture? These are some of the questions with which conservative theologians and apologists have continued to wrestle down to the present day.

The Warfield-Fuller Disagreement

Theologians at Princeton during the nineteenth century formulated an approach to such questions that was to become widely authoritative among conservative Protestants. In his *Systematic Theology* Charles Hodge declared that Scripture is "free from all error whether of doctrine, fact or precept."[1] The inspiration of Scripture, Hodge stated, is not confined to moral and religious truths but extends to the statement of facts, whether scientific, historical, or geographical.[2]

The formulation of Charles Hodge on inerrancy received further refinement in an 1881 article on "Inspiration" by A. A. Hodge and B. B. Warfield published in *The Presbyterian Review.* This statement by Hodge and Warfield is still considered by many conservative Protestants to be a definitive expression of the doctrine of biblical inerrancy:

> The historical faith of the church has always been, that all the affirmations of Scripture whether of spiritual doctrine or duty, or of physical or historical fact, or of psychological or philosophical principle, are without any error, when the *ipsissima verba* of the original autographs are ascertained and interpreted in their natural and intended sense.[3]

The reference to the original autographs recognized the existence of textual variants and corruptions; scientific and historical statements were to be interpreted in "their

---

1. Charles Hodge, *Systematic Theology* (Grand Rapids: Wm. B. Eerdmans, 1975 reprint), vol. 1, p. 152.
2. Ibid., p. 163.
3. Archibald A. Hodge and Benjamin B. Warfield, "Inspiration," *The Presbyterian Review* (April 1881), p. 238. This was reprinted in 1979 by Baker Book House, p. 28.

natural and intended sense." This matter of the "natural and intended sense" will, as we shall see, be a crucial consideration in the discussion of inerrancy and scientific truth.

Not all conservatives have been satisfied with the Hodge-Warfield formulation of inerrancy. Daniel P. Fuller, for example, has recently argued that doctrinal verses such as II Timothy 3:16 imply inerrancy with respect to "revelational knowledge," but not with respect to non-revelational matters of scientific fact:

> Let us observe that when the doctrinal verses teach or imply inerrancy, it is always in connection with revelational knowledge, not in connection with knowledge which makes a man wise to botany, meteorology, cosmology, or paleontology, i.e., to knowledge which is non-revelational simply because it is readily accessible to men . . . is it not at least as reasonable to infer from inspiration that the God who lovingly willed to communicate revelational truth to men deliberately accommodated his language in non-revelational matters to the way the original readers viewed the world about them, so as to enhance the communication of revelational truth, by which alone men could be saved?[4]

Fuller's proposed corrective to Warfield is based on a distinction between "revelational" and "non-revelational" content in Scripture. In non-revelational matters, inspiration involves an accommodation to the thought forms of the original readers.[5] This, in Fuller's view, can still be consistent with the verbal and *plenary* inspiration of Scripture. The presence of minor scientific errors in the Bible, in this view, would simply be an accommodation to human limitations, rather than a threat to plenary inspiration and authority.

Both Warfield and Fuller recognize that certain biblical

---

4. Daniel P. Fuller, "Benjamin B. Warfield's View of Faith and History," *Bulletin of the Evangelical Theological Society* 11 (1968), p. 81.
5. Ibid., p. 82.

statements dealing with the natural order create some difficulties for the modern reader accustomed to thinking in the categories of contemporary science. The difference in the two positions is found in the way in which these difficulties are treated. For Fuller, accommodation in nonrevelational matters can mean that actual scientific errors are not considered inconsistent with verbal, plenary inspiration. For Warfield, there may be scientific difficulties in the Bible, but not actual scientific errors, provided the text is properly interpreted in the "natural and intended sense." Warfield and Fuller do not disagree about the presence of scientific difficulties, but they do disagree about whether any such difficulties amount to actual errors. Thus in the matter of scientific accuracy, as in other areas of biblical authority, the question of inerrancy is really not so much about inspiration as it is about hermeneutics or interpretation. Perhaps a good deal of the acrimony that often surrounds discussions of inerrancy could be avoided if both sides of the debate recognized that neither the explicit doctrinal statements on inspiration nor the explicit scientific and historical difficulties automatically produce undebatable conclusions concerning inerrancy. Both positions make certain inferences on the basis of prior hermeneutical decisions. Both Christian charity and common sense dictate that all parties in the debate on inerrancy be willing to acknowledge the role that inferences and presuppositions play in their conclusions.

The position taken in this essay is that, in relation to scientific matters, Warfield's position is more satisfactory than Fuller's. The suggested distinction between revelational and non-revelational content seems, in the last analysis, artificial. While Fuller's position has the merit of emphasizing the central redemptive purpose of Scripture, the Scripture nowhere abstracts this redemptive intent from actual human history and the natural order. When the Scripture is understood in the "natural and intended sense," it is possible to acknowledge the central redemptive thrust of the Bible without charging the biblical writers with actual scientific error.

In matters of science and Scripture, the key to proper interpretation is recognizing that the "natural and intended sense" of Scripture in relation to science and history does not necessarily mean a *literal* sense in the manner of a photographic likeness. Scientific and historical facts can be presented in popular, figurative, and symbolic form—and still be just as factual as a more literal account. Conservative interpreters need not assume that the "natural and intended sense" of a biblical passage presupposes a precise photographic likeness of the historical or scientific realities in question. In order to illustrate this hermeneutical approach to the question of inerrancy and scientific fact, a case study of a particular scientific problem growing out of the biblical text will be attempted: the problem of the antiquity of man in relation to Genesis 3 and 4.

The Antiquity of Man

Ever since the publication in 1890 of William Henry Green's classic article "Primeval Chronology," which demonstrated that the genealogies of Genesis were not strict father-son relationships,[6] it has been commonly acknowl-

6. W. H. Green, "Primeval Chronology," *Bibliotheca Sacra* 47 (1890), pp. 285–303. For recent conservative thought on evolution see W. L. Craig, "Evangelicals and Evolution: An Analysis of the Debate Between the Creation Research Society and the American Scientific Affiliation," *Journal of the Evangelical Theological Society* 17 (1974), pp. 131–48. The CRS argues for a literal six-day creation, a relatively young earth, and the special creation of man around 10,000 B.C. Members of the ASA are divided on the question of evolution, but seem generally inclined toward nonliteral interpretations of Genesis. Competent evangelical opinion is presented in *Evolution and Christian Thought Today,* ed. Russell L. Mixter (Grand Rapids: Wm. B. Eerdmans, 1959). For a comprehensive survey of the voluminous material on evolution, see James R. Moore, "Evolutionary Theory and Christian Faith: A Bibliographical Guide to the Post-Darwin Controversies," *Christian Scholar's Review* 4 (1975), pp. 211–30.

edged that the precise antiquity of the human race cannot be determined from the Genesis genealogies. If geology and anthropology pointed to the origins of the race at 500,000 B.C. or earlier, this would create no theological difficulty; that is, if in fact the genealogies were not intended to supply information on the antiquity of the race. Green's conclusions seemed to preclude altogether the possibility of a conflict between science and Scripture at this point. Thus B. B. Warfield, writing in 1911, could confidently state:

> The question of the antiquity of man has of itself no theological significance. It is to theology, as such, a matter of entire indifference how long man has existed on earth. It is only because of the contrast which has been drawn between the short period which seems to be allotted to human history in the Biblic narrative, and the tremendously long period which certain schools of scientific speculation have assigned to the duration of human life on earth, that theology has become interested in the topic at all.[7]

Warfield argued that, in the light of Green's conclusions, conservative exegetes were no longer committed to defend Archbishop Ussher's chronology, according to which the world was created in 4004 B.C. Conservatives, Warfield argued, had nothing to fear from any discoveries pointing to the great antiquity of man. The matter appeared to be closed, and for the next forty years there was no significant advance in the discussion beyond Warfield's position of 1911.

In 1954 Bernard Ramm drew attention to a difficulty that heretofore had received little attention from conservative interpreters. With the geological and anthropological evidence pointing to a date for the antiquity of man on

7. Warfield, "On the Antiquity and the Unity of the Human Race," in *Biblical and Theological Studies,* ed. Samuel Craig (Philadelphia: Presbyterian and Reformed, 1952), p. 238; this was reprinted from the *Princeton Theological Review* 9 (1911), pp. 1–25.

the order of 500,000 B.C. or earlier, what was one to make of the transition from Genesis 3 to Genesis 4, where the immediate descendants of Adam already exhibit a highly developed level of culture?

> The chief problem with an origin of man at 500,000 B.C. is the connection of Gen. 3 with Gen. 4. We might stretch the tables of ancestors a few thousand years, but can we stretch them 200,000 years? In the fourth and fifth chapters of Genesis we have lists of names, ages of people, towns, agriculture, metallurgy, and music. This implies the ability to write, to count, to build, to farm, to smelt, and to compose. Further, this is done by the immediate descendants of Adam. Civilization does not reveal any evidence of its existence till about 8000 B.C. or, to some, 16,000 B.C. . . . It is problematic to interpret Adam as having been created at 200,000 B.C. or earlier, with civilization not coming into existence till say 8000 B.C.[8]

Ramm acknowledged the difficulty of the problem, but was content to leave it temporarily unresolved, pending further insights from exegesis and anthropology.

In a 1967 article in *Faith and Thought* the evangelical anthropologist James O. Buswell, III, comprehensively surveyed the discussions on the antiquity of the human race which were presented after Ramm's study.[9] Buswell pointed to a number of assumptions which have influenced various interpretations of Genesis texts: (1) that Adam is the first man, both theologically and anthropologically, and that all men are his physical descendants; (2) that Cain and Abel are individuals and the immediate

---

8. Bernard Ramm, *The Christian View of Science and Scripture* (Grand Rapids: Wm. B. Eerdmans, 1954), p. 228. Cf. the earlier comments by William A. Smalley and Marie Fetzer in *Modern Science and Christian Faith* (Wheaton, IL: Van Kampen Press, 1950), pp. 185-87.

9. James O. Buswell, III, "Genesis, the Neolithic Age, and the Antiquity of Adam," *Faith and Thought* 96 (1967), pp. 3-23. A popular version of this same article, "Adam and Neolithic Man," appeared in *Eternity*, February 1967, pp. 29ff.

descendants of Adam, and that the men of Genesis 4:17–24 are the immediate descendants of Cain; (3) that references to tilling of the ground and keeping of sheep (Gen. 4:2), city building (Gen. 4:17), tents and cattle (Gen. 4:20), musical instruments (Gen. 4:21), and instruments of bronze and iron (Gen. 4:22) point to a Neolithic level of culture; (4) that Neolithic culture was developed only after Paleolithic culture; (5) that the flood destroyed all mankind except Noah's family; (6) that the dates for the antiquity of fossil men are generally reliable.[10] An adequate solution for the problem of the antiquity of man requires careful examination of these assumptions.

Regarding assumption number (6), Buswell writes: "We have clear and unequivocal evidence for the existence of man—man who walked completely upright, who had human society and human culture, who buried his dead with ceremony; men who, in the opinion of many, must have been the descendants of Adam—at least 50,000 years ago."[11] Six adult Neanderthal skeletons from the Shanidar Cave in northern Iraq, studied by four different laboratories and given duplicate checks, yielded dates between 48,000 and 44,000 B.C.[12] While the cultural levels of Swanscombe man (c. 200,000 B.C.), *Homo erectus* (c. 300,000 B.C.), and *Australopithecinae* (c. 500,000 B.C.) are still matters of considerable debate among anthropologists, theologically the question of whether Adam is to be dated at 50,000 B.C. or 500,000 B.C. (or even earlier[13]) is almost immaterial, since in either case the difficulty of the gap between Genesis 3 and Genesis 4 seems acute. The present writer tends to agree with Buswell's position that the biblical Adam must be identified with the first

10. Buswell, "Genesis," p. 7.
11. Ibid., p. 6.
12. Ibid., p. 5.
13. See Richard Leakey, "Skull 1470—New Clue to Earliest Man?" *National Geographic* 143 (1973), pp. 819–29, who argues for a date c. 3,000,000 B.C.

man anthropologically, and that this first true man appeared at least 50,000 years ago.

In connection with assumption number (1), Buswell cites the study of J. M. Clark, who suggests a pre-Adamite hypothesis.[14] Clark postulates a distinction between the creation of the first men (Gen. 1:26) and the creation of Adam in Eden. The consequences of Adam's sin then "operate backwards in time as well as forwards, in the same way as the saving work of Christ. Thus men who lived long before Adam would be under the same dominion of sin and death as those who have lived since."[15] Exegetically this approach seems questionable, inasmuch as Genesis 1:26, 5:1, and 9:6 seem to assume that from the beginning there was a basic continuity of men created in the image and likeness of God, and Genesis 3:20 explicitly calls Eve the mother of "all living."

Buswell[16] also cites the articles of J. Stafford Wright,[17] T. C. Mitchell,[18] and James Murk[19] in relation to the first assumption. Wright argues that all fossil men prior to Neolithic times are "pre-Adamic" creatures.[20] But unlike Clark, Wright holds that these pre-Adamic creatures are not bearers of the image and do not have the status of men in the biblical sense.[21] He questions the existence of any firm evidence for religious beliefs in the Paleolithic age.[22]

---

14. J. M. Clark, "Genesis and Its Underlying Realities," *Faith and Thought* 93 (1964), pp. 146–58. For a discussion of earlier pre-Adamite theories, see Ramm, *Science and Scripture,* p. 221.

15. Clark, "Genesis," p. 154.

16. Buswell, "Genesis," p. 9.

17. J. Stafford Wright, "An Examination of Evidence for Religious Beliefs of Paleolithic Man," *Faith and Thought* 90 (1958), pp. 4–15.

18. T. C. Mitchell, "Archeology and Genesis I-XI," *Faith and Thought* 91 (1959), pp. 28–49.

19. James Murk, "Evidence for a Late Pleistocene Creation of Man," *Journal of the American Scientific Affiliation* 17 (1965), pp. 37–49.

20. Wright, "Religious Beliefs of Paleolithic Man," p. 14.

21. Ibid.

22. Ibid.

Both Mitchell and Murk also hold that the early fossil men were not truly "man" in the biblical sense of the term.[23] Buswell points out that purely spiritual criteria do not fossilize, and that, consequently, broader cultural criteria for the "human" are more reliable guides, and, in places like the Shanidar Cave, point back at least 50,000 years.[24]

With regard to assumptions (2) and (3), Buswell notes the suggestion of F. K. Farr that the references to Cain in Genesis 4 might represent the condensation of a number of ancient traditions associated with several individuals: Cain, the son of Adam; Cain, the first murderer; and Cain, the city builder and head of a line of patriarchs.[25] On such a reading the Cain of Genesis 4 would represent a conflation of several traditions, each preserving genuine historical reminiscences from the primeval era. Such a conjecture, which postulates a considerable period of time between Cain the son of Adam and Cain the first murderer, would offer plausible answers to the perennial questions of why Cain was afraid of being slain (Gen. 4:15) and where he obtained his wife (Gen. 4:17). On this view, the tradition of a later Cain presupposes the growth of population since the beginning. This suggestion, which in some ways is quite attractive, admittedly seems to have little support in the text. A straightforward reading of Genesis 4:1–16 would not appear to suggest a clear distinction between Cain the son of Adam and Cain the first murderer. On purely internal considerations, the suggestion seems difficult. Nevertheless, it could be that, in the total context of the anthropological and chronological considerations involved here, the suggestion of Farr, or one analogous to it, would be judged tenable.[26]

---

23. Mitchell, "Archeology," pp. 47, 49; Murk, "Late Pleistocene Creation of Man," pp. 43–47.

24. Buswell, "Genesis," p. 10.

25. F. K. Farr, "Cain," *International Standard Bible Encyclopedia* (1915), vol. I, p. 539.

26. Perhaps there might be an analogy here with the interpretation of the days of Genesis 1. Even though a straightforward reading of Genesis 1 in con-

With regard to assumption (3), the presumed Neolithic cultural level of Genesis 4, Buswell notes the argument of Mitchell that these features are of such a general nature as not to be limited to the Neolithic at all. Mitchell's argument is quoted extensively here:

> Enoch's "city," *ir,* need not be more than a small settlement, and could suggest equally a village farming settlement of the Near East, or one of the Upper Paleolithic mammoth hunter type, and the lot of Cain as wanderer would seem to bear this out. Jabal is described as the "father" or "originator" of those who dwell in tents and have cattle, but *miqneh* need not mean more than "possessions," or even possibly, if the Masoretic vocalization is ignored, it might be a form of *qaneh,* "reed," with a prefixed *mem* local, and have some such meaning as who "dwell in tents and places of reeds," that is reed, or wattle huts. This situation could relate to nomads in the hinterland of civilization, or Upper Paleolithic hut dwellers. The same could be said for the other four elements. *Kinnor* could mean basically, "a stringed instrument," and the presence, now generally accepted, of the archer's bow in the Upper Paleolithic opens up the possibility of the simple musical bow in that period. . . . The statement in 4:22 can legitimately be translated to mean "the sharpener of every cutter (or cutting implement) of copper and iron." Since both native copper and meteoric iron have presumably occurred on the surface from Paleolithic times, and both can be worked by grinding (being softer than stone), it seems unnecessary to regard this as evidence of metallurgy.[27]

Mitchell's suggestions, if correct, would remove to a considerable extent the difficulty of the gap between Genesis 3 and 4 by denying any strict identification of Genesis 4 with a Neolithic or later level of civilization. This approach

---

junction with Exodus 20:11 might suggest ordinary days of twenty-four hours, it is well known that many evangelical scholars hold a nonliteral interpretation of these days. The references to Cain in Hebrews 11:4 and I John 3:12, while offering no support for the conjecture, would not seem to rule it out completely, either, if there were other considerations pointing in that direction.

27. Mitchell, "Archeology," pp. 41–42.

seems to be a bit problematic, however, if one takes seriously the genuinely historical character of revelation: the revelation is mediated through the language and categories of the writer's own time and culture, not through the categories and cultural forms tens of thousands of years removed. It seems rather clear that the intent of Genesis 4:1–22, furthermore, plausibly reflects the cultural environment of the second millennium B.C. The primeval past is seen from the viewpoint of the second millennium, just as the distant future is seen through contemporary categories and images by the prophetic writers and the author of Revelation. For supporting evidence note that the explicit reference in Joshua 24:2 to the polytheistic worship of Abraham's ancestors makes it seem rather unlikely that the traditions of primeval history, integrally bound up as they are with Israel's redemptive relationship to Yahweh, are to be understood as having been handed down in their present form for tens of thousands of years prior to Moses.[28] Rather, these traditions are stamped with the faith of Abraham, and reflect the level of cultural and historical experience of the Abrahamic and post-Abrahamic era. Consequently, the removal of the gap between Genesis 3 and 4 by extending the cultural categories of Genesis 4:17–22 back into the Paleolithic[29] seems problematic.

In 1969 E. K. Victor Pearce, an English anthropologist

---

28. Cf. R. A. F. Mackenzie, "Before Abraham Was. . . ," *Catholic Biblical Quarterly* 15 (1953), pp. 131–40; Henricus Renckens, *Israel's Concept of the Beginning* (New York: Herder and Herder, 1964).

29. For this type of suggestion, see also J. O. Buswell, Jr., *A Systematic Theology of the Christian Religion* (Grand Rapids: Zondervan, 1962), vol. I, pp. 365–68. To the suggestion that Cain and Abel might only *appear* to be domesticators of plants and animals, Paul Seely replies: "But Moses could write of *hunting* (Gen. 25:27; 27:3, 30) and *gathering* (Ex. 16:16; Num. 15:32). Couldn't he have described the *hunting* and *gathering* economy of Paleolithic times? If Genesis 2–4 is literal history, why should Moses make a Paleolithic culture look so very Neolithic?" ("Adam and Anthropology: A Proposed Solution," *Journal of the American Scientific Affiliation* 22 [1970], p. 88).

who is an evangelical Christian, presented a new case for a variation of the pre-Adamite hypothesis.[30] Pearce's hypothesis, if valid, would offer a solution to the problem of the gap between Genesis 3 and 4. Pearce argues that the cultural references in Genesis 2–4 act as a type of "cultural fossil zone" and date Adam as a New Stone Age farmer.[31] The men of Genesis 1, on the other hand, in Pearce's view represent the Paleolithic type of hunter-gatherer culture.[32] In contrast to some earlier pre-Adamite views, Pearce argues that the man of Genesis 2 has no genetic connection with the men of Genesis 1, but in fact represents a *de novo* creation. Pearce contends that the present *Homo sapiens* (modern-type man), dating from approximately 30,000 years ago, is not directly descended from *Homo neanderthalensis* (c. 150,000–40,000 years ago), or from Swanscombe man (c. 200,000 B.C.), or *Homo erectus* (c. 300,000 B.C.), or *Australopithecinae* (c. 500,000 B.C.).[33] This assumption of a hiatus between *Homo neanderthalensis* and modern *Homo sapiens* (and therefore between Gen. 1 and 2) is seriously questioned by Paul Seely in a response to Pearce.[34] Seely claims that "the overwhelming majority of anthropologists today, if not all of them, would concur in saying that in spite of some sites which show hiatuses, there is no 10,000 year hiatus or any other ultimate hiatus or temporal discontinuity between Neanderthal man and modern man."[35] Pearce's proposed discontinuity between the men of Genesis 1 and the men of Genesis 2–4 can thus be questioned on anthropological grounds. As we have

30. E. K. Victor Pearce, *Who Was Adam?* (London: Paternoster Press, 1969). His thesis is also presented in "Proto-neolithic Adam and Recent Anthropology," *Journal of the American Scientific Affiliation* 23 (1971), pp. 130–39.

31. Pearce, *Who Was Adam?*, p. 22.

32. Ibid., p. 34.

33. Ibid., p. 42.

34. Paul Seely, "Not a Viable Theory," *Journal of the American Scientific Affiliation* 23 (1971), pp. 132–36.

35. Ibid., p. 135.

already seen, pre-Adamite hypotheses also run aground on the implied continuity of the divine image in Genesis 1:26, 5:1, and 9:6, and the statement in 3:20 that Eve was the mother of "all living." Consequently, Pearce's work, though it contains fruitful insights and a wealth of valuable anthropological information, does not appear to offer a convincing solution to the problem of Genesis 3 and 4.

Hermeneutical Issues

Having surveyed some significant evangelical discussions on the implications of anthropology for the integration of the early Genesis history, we might consider now some broader hermeneutical issues. The present writer is of the opinion that it is important to avoid a "purely literal" versus "purely symbolic" dichotomy in relation to the historicity of the early chapters of Genesis in general and Genesis 3–4 in particular. Both the form-critical studies of Genesis undertaken in the light of the extrabiblical literature of the ancient Near East[36] and the discoveries of modern anthropology indicate that the historical character of the Genesis texts must be understood on its own terms, and not on the basis of a priori notions of what historical writing ought to be. In view of both liberal and neoorthodox denials of the historical value of the Genesis accounts, it is quite understandable that conserva-

36. The literature dealing with possible extrabiblical parallels to the Genesis creation narratives is, of course, enormous. The present writer makes no pretense of having addressed this entire area. For a helpful survey from a conservative perspective, see Walter C. Kaiser, Jr., "The Literary Form of Genesis 1–11," in *New Perspectives on the Old Testament,* ed. J. Barton Payne (Waco, TX: Word Books, 1970), pp. 48–65; cf. John L. McKenzie, "The Literary Characteristics of Genesis 2–3," *Theological Studies* 15 (1954), pp. 541–72; W. G. Lambert, "A New Look at the Babylonian Background of Genesis," *Journal of Theological Studies,* n.s. 16 (1965), pp. 287–300; Gerhard Hasel, "The Polemic Nature of the Genesis Cosmology," *Evangelical Quarterly* 46 (1974), pp. 81–102.

tives would be especially insistent to affirm their historical content. The danger here, as in any polemical situation, is that a theological "hardening of the categories" can occur which excludes a more nuanced and mediating position. Why must the early history in Genesis be either purely literal or purely symbolic? Such a dichotomy seems to be presupposed in the hermeneutical stance of the conservative Lutheran theologian David P. Scaer. In connection with the historicity of Genesis 1–3, Scaer argues that "either the entire account is symbolical, including the reference to God, or the account is historical or real, not only in the section referring to God but also the section dealing with the serpent."[37] In this view the *historical* and the *symbolic* seem to be understood as mutually exclusive categories. But, in the long history of the church, this view is only one of several possible understandings of the relationship between symbol and historical event.

In 1913 Joseph Feldmann offered a comprehensive survey of the history of the interpretation of Genesis 2 and 3.[38] Feldmann divides the schools of interpretation into five major categories. These categories, with major figures holding the particular views, are as follows: the "literalistic-historical" view (later Augustine, Luther, Calvin, Grotius, Gerhard, Quenstedt, Calovius, Keil, Hengstenberg); the "allegorical" view (Philo, Clement of Alexandria, Origen, earlier Augustine, Rupert of Deutz); the "historical-allegorical" view, combining literal and allegorical elements (Gregory the Great, Athanasius, Gregory of Nazianzus, Gregory of Nyssa, Chrysostom, John of Damascus, Abelard, Aquinas); the "mythical" view (Kant,

37. David P. Scaer, "The Problems of Inerrancy and Historicity in Connection with Genesis 1–3," *Concordia Theological Quarterly* 41 (1977), pp. 20–25. Scaer does not deal with the data of anthropology, the problem of Genesis 3–4, or the possible relevance of extrabiblical data as clues to literary form.

38. Joseph Feldmann, *Paradies und Sündenfall* (Münster, 1913), pp. 501–605. Feldmann also presents a comprehensive review of extrabiblical parallels, pp. 60–500.

Eichhorn, Schelling, de Wette, Hegel, Wellhausen, Gunkel); the "historical-folklore" view (Feldmann),[39] that is, the view that historical reminiscences have been preserved in the form of popular, folk history or *Volkstradition.* Feldmann was writing, of course, prior to the rise of neoorthodoxy, but it would appear that his fourth and fifth categories have real affinity with the interpretations offered by this movement.[40] Feldmann's survey indicates that the literal-historical view has not been the only position held by orthodox writers. In particular, the historical-allegorical view had rather wide acceptance in the Eastern Church. In the light of the Reformation's reactions to medieval allegorizing, and nineteenth- and twentieth-century conservative reactions to liberal and neoorthodox attacks on the historical value of Genesis, it seems all the more important to recall the history of interpretation, in order to formulate a properly balanced position.

It is also to be remembered that within the broader conservative tradition itself, a significant number of writers during recent centuries have seen no conflict between a high doctrine of Scripture and the recognition of symbolic elements in the early chapters of Genesis. In 1889 Franz Delitzsch wrote:

> Granting even that the trees of Paradise and the serpent were mere symbols, this much is still left, that man fell away from that first good development which was implanted in him through the temptation of Satan . . . even if the form

---

39. Ibid., pp. 574–86.

40. For representative neoorthodox treatments of creation and fall, see Karl Barth, *Church Dogmatics* III.1, *The Doctrine of Creation* (Edinburgh: T. & T. Clark, 1958), pp. 42ff. ("saga"); Emil Brunner, *The Christian Doctrine of Creation and Redemption* (Philadelphia: Westminster Press, 1952), pp. 3–45; Paul Tillich, *Systematic Theology* (Chicago: University of Chicago Press, 1967), vol. II, pp. 39–44; Dietrich Bonhoeffer, *Creation and Fall* (London: SCM Press, 1959); Reinhold Niebuhr, *The Nature and Destiny of Man* (New York: Charles Scribner's Sons, 1941), vol. I, pp. 260ff.

of the narrative is regarded as mythic or symbolic, the serpent was pre-eminently adapted to represent an earthly power of seduction with a mysterious background.[41]

In 1943, Albertus Pieters, professor of Bible and missions at Western Theological Seminary of the Reformed Church in America, in his *Notes on Genesis* adopted a symbolic interpretation of the temptation narrative:

> The actual event and supremely important truth presented here in symbolic form (just as what really happened to the kings of Judah is so presented in Ezekiel 19), is that man was created innocent, lived in that state for a time . . . was tempted, and fell. To set this before us, the writer takes the already existing serpent, his writhing and sinuous approach, and the hatred commonly felt for him, and uses these things as pictures of spiritual realities. The alleged cunning of the serpent, his talking, the eating of the fruit of a tree, the aprons, the hiding in the bushes, the coats of skins, the cherubim, the naive call and conversation, etc., etc. are then all things that did not actually happen, but are part of the pictorial representation.[42]

In Pieter's view, then, the temptation and fall are actual historical events, but are represented in symbolic form.

More recently, Bernard Ramm has expressed the belief that the proper interpretation of the creation narratives is to be found somewhere in the territory between the strict literalism of many conservatives and the nonhistorical, "existential" view of a neoorthodox theologian such as Emil Brunner.[43] J. I. Packer has admitted the difficulty of drawing hard and fast boundaries between the literal and the symbolic in the early chapters of Genesis.[44] The conserva-

---

41. Franz Delitzsch, *A New Commentary on Genesis* (New York: Scribner and Welford, 1889), vol. I, pp. 150–51.

42. Albertus Pieters, *Notes on Genesis* (Grand Rapids: Wm. B. Eerdmans, 1943), p. 100.

43. Ramm, *Science and Scripture,* pp. 222, 224.

44. J. I. Packer, *Fundamentalism and the Word of God* (Grand Rapids: Wm. B. Eerdmans, 1969), p. 98.

tive Old Testament scholar R. K. Harrison has suggested that the concept of "religious drama" might be an appropriate categorization for the narratives of the creation and fall.[45] The foregoing survey would certainly indicate that the conservative tradition is by no means locked into a strictly literalistic hermeneutic at this point.

Some further considerations of a philosophical nature also indicate that the antithesis "purely literal" versus "purely symbolic" with reference to historicity is in fact an unnecessary hermeneutical dichotomy. Recent discussions in the philosophy of science concerning scientific models, and in the philosophy of language about the "picture theory of meaning," challenge a widely-held assumption that meaningful speech about the real world must "picture" reality in a photographic sense of the term. We will examine rather briefly both lines of discussion.

In the philosophy of science it has recently become common to distinguish between *replica* and *analogue* models.[46] A model is a mechanical or theoretical construct which enables the investigator to reproduce and manipulate selected features of a complex reality in terms of experiences, categories, and materials more familiar to him. A replica or scale model is simply a scaled-down reproduction of the object in question—a model airplane prepared for a wind tunnel test, for example. An analogue model, on the other hand, is not a literal "picture" of the reality which it represents. A vibrating-spring model of an electrical circuit, the Bohr planetary model of the hydrogen atom, and a computer program simulating the behavior of the American economy are all analogue models which do not "picture" in any strictly literal way the realities they

45. R. K. Harrison, *Introduction to the Old Testament* (Grand Rapids: Wm. B. Eerdmans, 1969), p. 556.

46. Cf. Mary Hesse, "Models and Analogy in Science," *Encyclopedia of Philosophy* 5 (1967), pp. 354–58. Also helpful are Max Black, *Models and Metaphors: Studies in Language and Philosophy* (Ithaca, NY: Cornell University Press, 1962), and Ian T. Ramsey, *Models and Mystery* (London: Oxford University Press, 1964).

represent. There exists an isomorphism or structural analogy between elements of the model and the corresponding elements of the reality represented, but the model is not intended to be a photographic likeness. A hydrogen atom, for example, is not really like a miniaturized planetary system, but rather a physical reality having certain electromagnetic properties which can be adequately described only in the mathematical language of quantum mechanics. The mental images associated with the concepts of "wave" and "particle" are not fully adequate to describe the subatomic phenomena so far removed from our ordinary range of experience. In relation to our particular discussions, it is important to realize the distinction between the two types of models, and also to realize that neither is intrinsically more truthful than the other. Whether a replica ("pictorial") or an analogue ("nonpictorial") model is more appropriate is simply a question of the nature of the field in question. The further removed the object is from our normal range of experience, the more necessary it is to use analogue models. If this is the case with certain physical realities, we should certainly be prepared to examine the possibility of nonliteral representations of realities in the spiritual realm.

Recent studies in the philosophy of language have challenged the "picture theory of meaning," which seems to imply that meaningful language must in some sense be a pictorial representation of that to which the language refers. The so-called picture theory of meaning, represented by the work of Bertrand Russell and the earlier Wittgenstein, and developed by logical positivists such as Hans Reichenbach and A. J. Ayer, was challenged by the later Wittgenstein and by J. L. Austin.[47] The tendency in positivism was to limit meaningful statements to those of a purely logical, mathematical, or empirically verifiable na-

---

47. Cf. Jerry H. Gill, *The Possibility of Religious Knowledge* (Grand Rapids: Wm. B. Eerdmans, 1971), pp. 93ff.

ture, where empirical verification was understood in terms of the paradigm of the laboratory sciences. Obviously, in terms of such a theory, the cognitive status of such concepts as "God," "justice," "duty," and "soul" is in doubt. In his later work Wittgenstein became increasingly dissatisfied with the positivist criterion of meaning, and developed a theory of language in which meaning was seen not merely as the representation of logical or empirical objects. Language mediated man's experience of a multidimensional reality, a reality which could not be limited to the world of science and mathematics. In such a view, language about religious and moral experience, while *mediated* through empirical objects, is not *reducible* to pictorial representations of empirical objects. To illustrate from quite a different context: it has been argued that the Eucharistic words, "This is my body," refer to an invisible spiritual reality (the saving benefits of the death of Christ), a reality mediated through sensory experience but not reducible to it. The meaning of the statement, "This is my body," is anchored in the invisible spiritual reality, not in the bread itself; the visible bread is the *medium* or vehicle but not the *terminus* of the meaning-content of the statement.

We will now attempt to draw together the foregoing lines of discussion and make an application to the problem of Genesis 3 and 4. The suggestion to be made is that the events of Genesis 3 and 4 are to be understood in terms of a "redemptive-historical model."[48] The early Genesis narratives *model* historical realities after the fashion of an analogue model: there is a genuine structural correspondence between the features of the model and the historical realities which mediate the spiritual content, but this correspondence is not understood in terms of literal pictorial representation. The postulation of an *analogue*

48. The same could apply to Genesis 1–4 generally.

rather than a replica model is in keeping with the circumstance that the reality in question is quite removed from the range of our normal experience. Descriptions of the very small (the Bohr model of the atom), the end of history (the Book of Revelation), and the beginnings of history (early Genesis) all transcend our normal experience, and our normal spatiotemporal categories must be stretched whenever we attempt to represent such realities.

In this view such features of the narrative as the trees in the garden, the serpent, and the chronological framework (civilization is highly developed already in the second generation), are understood as *modeling* historical events, but not in the sense of photographic identity. In terms of the chronological connection between Genesis 3 and 4, the relation between the time frame of the narrative/model and the time frame of external history is not understood to be "one-for-one" but rather "telescopic" in nature.[49] The interpretation of Genesis 3 and 4 being proposed here takes the text neither as "myth" nor as a literal photographic likeness of the historical events. Unlike Reinhold Niebuhr, this interpretation does not consider the fall as mythical and purely symbolic. In Niebuhr's words:

> Christian theology has found it difficult to refute the rationalistic rejection of the myth of the Fall without falling into the literalistic error of insisting upon the Fall as an historical event. . . . When the Fall is made an event in history rather than a symbol of an aspect of every historical moment in the life of man, the relation of evil to goodness in that moment is obscured.[50]

---

49. This is quite in keeping with the nature of the genealogies of Genesis, as demonstrated by W. H. Green in the last century. The same transformation of the chronological scale is evident in day-age hypotheses relative to Genesis 1.

50. Reinhold Niebuhr, *The Nature and Destiny of Man,* vol. 1, pp. 267–68, 269. The position of Paul Tillich is quite similar: "Theology must clearly and unambiguously represent 'the Fall' as a symbol for the human situation universally, not as the story of an event that happened 'once upon a time' " (*Systematic Theology,* vol. II, p. 29).

In contrast to the view that the fall is a myth, the features of the model being proposed have a real connection with the particular events of external, space-time reality; in contrast to strictly literal views, the features of the model are not understood in terms of a simple photographic likeness. The model describes, through figurative means, the actual flow of human history from the beginning.[51]

In closing, a number of tentative conclusions concerning the interpretation of Genesis 3 and 4 in terms of a redemptive-historical model will be listed:

1. The narratives concern the actual, historical parents of the human race who were tempted by Satan, and who, through their fall, plunged the entire race into sin and death.
2. Features of the narrative such as the trees in the garden and the serpent may be visual representations of invisible, spiritual realities.
3. In Genesis 3 and 4 there is a "telescoping" of the chronological framework, that is, of the time span from the first generation to the development of civilization.
4. The cultural level implied by Genesis 4 is at least Neolithic, and in fact represents the general cultural experience of the second millennium B.C. through which the primeval history is retrospectively interpreted.
5. The Adam of Genesis represents the first human being, both theologically and anthropologically. True human beings have existed on earth at least since the Neanderthals (c. 50,000 B.C.), and quite likely for much longer.
6. Consequently, the conceptions of human origins as presented by Genesis and by anthropology, when both are

51. Cf. Ezekiel 19, where the history of the princes of Israel is narrated in figurative form. The temptation accounts of Matthew 4 and Luke 4 imply real events in the life of our Lord, but do not necessarily imply that Satan appeared in a literal physical form, or that Jesus was transported literally to the pinnacle of the temple. Intangible spiritual realities (e.g., temptation) are mediated through visual imagery ("modeled") for the sake of communication. The "redemptive-historical model" view is similar in some respects to Barth's concept of "saga," but unlike Barth, it stresses the real causal link between our sin and the sin of the first man (cf. *Christian Dogmatics* IV.1, pp. 508–13).

properly understood, are not in contradiction, but form a complementary whole.

These, then, are the tentative conclusions of our case study of Genesis 3 and 4. The proposal for interpreting the text in terms of a redemptive-historical model is really an extension of the Hodge-Warfield principle of interpreting the text in the "natural and intended sense." The Scripture gives accurate and truthful information about science and history, but in a form appropriate to its own purposes. Those who hold to the inerrancy of Scripture have nothing to fear from honest scientific and historical research, for the Lord of nature and history is also the Lord of the Scriptures. This ultimate harmony of science and Scripture is exactly what both common sense and a living faith would lead us to expect.

GORDON D. FEE

7

Hermeneutics and Common Sense: An Exploratory Essay on the Hermeneutics of the Epistles

It has long been my conviction that the battle for inerrancy must be settled in the arena of hermeneutics. The basic differences that have emerged among evangelicals, for example, between those who believe in "limited" inerrancy[1] and those who believe in "unlimited" inerrancy, are not textual, but exegetical and hermeneutical. Unfortunately, a good deal of name-calling and mud-slinging has gone on over theological definitions of inerrancy, while exegetical and hermeneutical imprecision abounds.

This conviction has been supported most recently—unwittingly to be sure—by Harold Lindsell's *Battle for the*

1. "Limited" inerrancy describes the belief that what God intends to convey in Scripture, or the message of Scripture, is without error, but that this absence of error does not necessarily apply to the incidental scientific or historical notations in Scripture.

Bible. Early on he inveighs against those who would "destroy the idea of biblical infallibility neatly by providing interpretations of Scripture at variance with the plain reading of the texts."[2] Yet when he himself tries to resolve "the case of the missing thousand" (Num. 25:9; I Cor. 10:8), he does so with precisely the same kind of hermeneutical stance, that is, by abandoning "the plain reading of the texts" and inveighing against those who read Paul's account "superficially."[3]

The burden of this present essay is not necessarily to resolve the hermeneutical tensions highlighted by the battle for inerrancy. Nor does it aim to spell out the hermeneutical principles required by a belief in biblical inerrancy. Rather the essay intends to be more foundational and to offer some suggestions in the area of common sense. The plea is for greater hermeneutical precision in order to answer the thorny question of how to move from the first to the twentieth century without abandoning the plain sense of the texts, on the one hand, and yet without canonizing first-century culture, on the other.

I have chosen to limit my remarks in this essay to the New Testament Epistles. The reason for this is twofold: (1) the problem of "cultural relativity" and its relationship to inerrancy is most often raised here. (2) Many of the battle lines in the current debate have been drawn over the issues of women's role in the twentieth-century church. Here especially, hermeneutical precision—or at least consistency—has been lacking on both sides. Unfortu-

2. Harold Lindsell, *The Battle for the Bible* (Grand Rapids: Zondervan, 1976), p. 30.

3. Ibid., pp. 167–69. Lindsell's preferred "solution" is that both writers were rounding off the number 23,500. It is hard to believe that he really intends us to take this seriously. This might easily have been the case in Numbers. But how can Paul have possibly known that the real number was 23,500 when the only text he had already had rounded it off to 24,000? That is, the only way Paul could have rounded off the number 23,500 would have been for him to have access to that number!

nately, in an area where hermeneutics is in fact the key issue, some have taken such a rigid stance on the basis of their own hermeneutics that they have accused others of believing in an errant Bible because they do not hold to the same interpretation.

The Basic Problem

In his now famous article on "Biblical Theology" in the *Interpreter's Dictionary of the Bible,* Krister Stendahl suggested the core of the hermeneutical problem today to be the contrast between "What *did* Scripture mean when it was written?" (the aim of historical exegesis) and "What *does* it mean to us today?" Historical exegesis, of course, is the culprit. By insisting that we go back to the then and there, many exegetes seemed less concerned with the here and now. Exegesis became a historical discipline, pure and simple; and the Bible seemed less a Book for all seasons, an eternal Word from God, and more like a book of antiquity, full of the culture and religious idiosyncrasies of another day. A new way of "hearing" Scripture was forced upon us. How is a statement spoken to a given historical context, in response to a specific historical problem, the Word of God for us, whose context is so different? How, or when, does something that is culturally conditioned become transcultural?

These problems are especially acute for us in the evangelical tradition, where a real bifurcation has taken place. On the one hand, there are those who read the Epistles without a sense of the then and there. It is the eternal Word, which is therefore always here and now. Yet in practice it works out a little differently. For example, many evangelicals consider the imperative to Timothy, "Use a little wine for the sake of your stomach" (I Tim. 5:23, RSV), to be culturally and specifically bound. Water was unsafe to drink, we are told, so Timothy was to take wine for medical reasons. All of this might be true, but many of the same Christians insist that men today should not have long hair, because "nature itself teaches us" this (although it is seldom recognized that short hair is "natural" only as the result of a *non*-natural means—a haircut!). And we are *never* told how one arrives at such neat distinctions.

On the other hand, some of us who engage in historical exegesis do so at times with an uneasy conscience. We see a man like Ernst Käsemann engage in the same discipline with great expertise, but we are ill at ease with his "canon within the canon" (who decides on that inner canon?), which allows him to call the Gospel of John heterodox and say of Paul: "Being an apostle is no excuse for bad theology"! What is to keep us from the charge of picking and choosing when historical exegesis brings us face to face with statements and ideas that jar us in our twentieth-century ethos? How does the Word spoken then and there, to which we are theologically committed, become a Word to us today?

Because I am an exegete committed to the canon of Scripture as God's Word, I can neither reject exegesis (what it meant then) nor neglect hermeneutics (what does it say today).[4] But those of us who take such a stance have still further problems: (1) In the past two decades there has been a spate of literature, mostly by Roman Catholics, on the *sensus plenior* of Scripture, which is defined by R. E. Brown as "the deeper meaning, intended by God but not clearly intended by the human author, that is seen to exist in the words of Scripture when they are studied in the light of further revelation or of development in the understand-

---

4. These are not precise usages of the two terms, but I will tend to use them in this way in the present essay. *Exegesis* is in fact concerned with what the text *meant* in its historical context. *Hermeneutics* has to do with the science of interpretation in *all* of its ramifications. But since the term has to do especially with what a text *means* (which includes what is meant), I will use the term to refer to what the biblical text means for us in terms of our understanding and obedience.

ing of revelation."[5] Most evangelicals have avoided the term *sensus plenior,* since the concept of "development in the understanding of revelation" seems to leave the door open for the magisterium to define "God's intentions"; nonetheless, evangelicals use such terms as "secondary sense" to function in the same way as *sensus plenior.* The problem has to do with both the legitimacy of *sensus plenior* and, allowing its legitimacy, finding the principles for determining deeper meanings. (2) Protestant theologians have sometimes tended to lay aside the results of historical exegesis by distinguishing between the explicit and the implicit in Scripture, and have argued: "Therefore not only the express statements of Scripture, but its implication . . . must be regarded as the Word of God."[6] But again rules or principles are seldom given as to how one finds the implication of the Word of God.

I have neither the space nor the expertise to answer all the questions that I have raised, but we evangelicals must speak to them. So here are some suggestions. I begin by stating in detail what exegesis of the Epistles as epistles entails, and then move on to the implications.

Interpreting the Epistles

Traditionally for most Christians the Epistles seem to be the easiest parts of the New Testament to interpret. They are looked upon as so many propositions to be believed and imperatives to be obeyed. One need not be skilled in exegesis to understand that "all have sinned," or that "by grace are you saved through faith," or that "if any one is in Christ, he is a new creation." When we read, "Do all things

5. R. E. Brown, "Hermeneutics," in *The Jerome Bible Commentary* (Englewood Cliffs, NJ: Prentice-Hall, 1968), p. 616.

6. Louis Berkhof, *Principles of Biblical Interpretation,* 2nd ed. (Grand Rapids: Baker Book House, 1952), p. 159.

without grumbling or questioning," our difficulty is not with understanding, but with obeying. How, then, do the Epistles as epistles pose problems for interpretation?

The answer to that quickly becomes obvious when one leads a group of Christians through I Corinthians. "How is Paul's opinion (e.g., I Cor. 7:25: 'I have no command from the Lord, but I give a judgment as one who by the Lord's mercy is trustworthy,' NIV) to be taken as God's Word?" some will ask, especially when they personally dislike some of the implications of that opinion. And the questions continue. How does the excommunication of the brother in chapter 5 relate to today's church, especially when he can simply go down the street to another church? What is the point of chapters 12–14, if one is in a local church where charismatic gifts are not accepted as valid for the twentieth century? How do we "get around" the very clear implication in chapter 11:2–16 that women should have a head covering when they are praying and prophesying?

It becomes clear that the Epistles are not as easy to interpret as is often thought. What principles, then, apply specifically to this genre? Here are some suggestions:

Let us begin by noting that the Epistles themselves are not homogeneous. Many years ago Adolf Deissmann, on the basis of the vast papyrus discoveries, made a distinction between "letters" and "epistles."[7] The former, the "real letters" as he called them, were nonliterary, that is, not written for the public and posterity, but "intended only for the person or persons to whom [they were] addressed." In contrast to this is the "epistle," which is "an artistic literary form, a species of literature . . . intended for publicity." Deissmann himself considered all the Pauline Epistles as well as II and III John to be "real letters." Although William M. Ramsay cautioned us not "to reduce all the letters of the New Testament to one or other of these

7. *Light from the Ancient East,* 4th ed. (Grand Rapids: Baker Book House, 1965 reprint), pp. 146–245, especially pp. 228–45.

categories"[8]—in some instances it seems to be a question of more or less—the distinction is nevertheless a valid one. Romans and Philemon differ from one another not only in content but also in the degree to which they are occasional. And in contrast with any of Paul's letters, I Peter is far more an "epistle."

Further distinctions must also be drawn. For example, Hebrews is, as A. M. Hunter said, "three parts tract and one part letter."[9] But it is far more than a tract; it is an eloquent homily proclaiming the absolute superiority of Christ, interspersed with urgent words of exhortation. James, on the other hand, looks very little like a letter, but often very much like the wisdom literature of the Old Testament and Apocrypha, except that the wisdom literature is poetry and James is prose.

However diverse the Epistles might be, they nonetheless have one thing in common. They are occasional documents of the first century, written out of the context of the author to the context of the recipients. We are often, as it were, on one side of a telephone conversation and must piece together from this end what the other party is saying, or what his problem is. Or as R. P. C. Hanson said of II Corinthians: "As we read it, we sometimes feel as if we had turned on the [radio] in the middle of an elaborate play: characters are making most lively speeches and events of great interest and importance are happening, but we do not know who exactly the speakers are and we are not sure exactly what is happening."[10]

Moreover, all of this took place in the first century. Our difficulty here is that we are removed from them not only by so many years in time, and therefore in circumstances and culture, but also very often in the world of thought.

---

8. *Letters to the Seven Churches of Asia* (New York: A. C. Armstrong and Son, 1905), p. 24.

9. *Introducing the New Testament,* 2nd ed. (London: SCM Press, 1957), p. 157.

10. *II Corinthians* (London: SCM Press, 1954), p. 7.

Sound hermeneutics with regard to the Epistles, therefore, seems to require the following three steps:

1. *Understand as much as possible the original setting.* The interpreter, if you will, must remove his twentieth-century bifocals, shedding the filter of twentieth-century mentality, and put himself back into the first century. For the Epistles this has a double focus: (a) The interpreter must try as best he can to reconstruct the situation of the recipients. That is, he must ask, how is this letter, or this section of the letter, an answer to their problems or a response to their needs? In every case, a primary concern of interpretation is to try to hear what *they* would have heard. (b) He must try to live with the author and understand his mentality and his context. Above everything else the interpreter must try to understand what the author *intended* the recipients to hear.

A maxim of hermeneutics for the Epistles is: *The correct meaning of a passage must be something the author intended and his readers could have understood.* For example, it has often been suggested that the phrase "when the perfect comes" (I Cor. 13:10) refers to the completion of the canon of Scripture, and that therefore it points to the end of the first century as the time when charismatic gifts will cease. But surely that is altogether modern. Not only does the immediate context imply that the *eschaton* is intended (verse 12, "Now we see but a poor reflection; then we shall see face to face. Now I know in part; then I shall know fully, even as I am fully known," NIV), but there seems to be no way either that Paul could have meant the completion of the canon, or that the Corinthians would have so understood him.

2. *Hear the Word of God that is addressed to that situation.* This, of course, will be very closely tied to the first principle and sometimes they will be one. The point here is not that some parts of the Epistles are inspired and others are not, but rather that the recipients' context often reflects a problem which needs correcting or a lack of understand-

ing that needs enlightening. Our task is to discover (or "hear") the Word of God that was addressed to that situation, the Word that called for the recipients' obedience or brought them understanding.

3. *Hear that same Word as it is addressed to our situation.* Understandably enough, most of us want to go directly to this step, that is, to have Paul speak directly out of the first century into ours. This is not to suggest that such may not or cannot happen, but the point is that very often the words of the Epistles are culturally conditioned by the first-century setting.[11] If these words are going to be God's Word to us, then we must first of all hear what God's Word was to the original recipients. By being aware of God's message both to the first century and to us, we avoid two dangers. First, there is the danger that the words may never leave the first century. Some passages seem to address us, and some do not. If we have no one struggling with whether to join his pagan neighbors at feasts in an idol's temple, or no one denying the bodily resurrection, or if our culture does not insist on women's heads being covered, or if we have no one drunk at the Lord's table or shouting (by the "Spirit"), "Jesus is cursed," then the Epistles have historical interest at these points, but they scarcely address us.

The second danger is that the Epistles may never belong to the first century. In this case we suppose that every word comes directly to us. But sometimes that word is not God's *intended* Word to us! For example, if the intent of Paul's word about partaking of the Lord's Supper "unworthily" is to correct the abuses of divisiveness, gluttony, and drunkenness while at the Lord's table, then our ordinary application of that text to personal piety does not

11. In a certain sense, of course, every word of Scripture is culturally conditioned, in that, for example, every word of the New Testament was first spoken in the context of the first century. The degree of "cultural conditioning" is a relative matter, which will receive attention later in this paper.

seem to be God's *intended* Word. What was being said to *that* situation had to do with an attitude, or lack of it, toward the Lord's Supper itself. By their division and drunkenness the Corinthians were profaning the Supper, not "discerning the body," missing the whole point of it all. Surely the twentieth-century Christian needs to hear *that* Word, rather than a word about "getting rid of the sin in his life in order to be worthy to partake," which is foreign to the point of the passage.

If we are to escape both of these dangers, then we *must* discover what God said to that setting, and it is that Word which *we* must hear, even if we must hear it in a new setting or learn to recognize contemporary settings to which it should be addressed.

These principles may perhaps be best illustrated from a passage like I Corinthians 3:9b–17, which has been frequently misunderstood and misapplied, and has served as a theological battleground for a controversy to which Paul is not speaking at all.

It takes no great skill to recognize that the context of I Corinthians 3:9b–17 is partisan strife in the church at Corinth. In 1:10–12 Paul says that Chloe's people have told him all about the tendency to divide into cliques over favorite leaders. On either side of the immediate context (3:4–9a and 21–23) this strife is obviously still in view. Unless verses 9b–17 can be demonstrated to be a digression (and here they cannot), then one must assume them to speak directly to this problem.

Paul's response to the strife among the Corinthians is twofold. His first great concern is theological—their sloganeering and dividing on the basis of human leaders reflect on their understanding of salvation, as if men (especially men with great wisdom and eloquence) had something to do with it. So in 1:18—2:16 Paul reaffirms that salvation is God's business from start to finish; and, as though deliberately to leave men out of it, God wisely chose the foolishness of the cross as His means of accomplishing it, so that their trust (="boast") will not be in men but in God.

In chapter 3 Paul turns to the practical implications of the divisions. He begins with two analogies, intended to show the role of the human ministers in salvation. The particulars in both analogies are closely related (Paul plants/lays the foundation; Apollos waters/builds the superstructure; the Corinthian church is the field/building; God owns the field/building), but the point of each is considerably different. The agricultural analogy is intended to help the church have a proper perspective as to its leaders; they are servants, not lords. The figure from architecture (v. 10) turns the argument toward the leaders themselves; they are to take care how they build (the church is obviously the object being built). Verse 11 is simply a parenthesis reiterating the point of 1:18—2:16; namely, that Christ alone is the foundation of the church in Corinth. Verses 12-15 therefore have nothing to do with personal morality or piety, as to how one builds his own life on Christ. Rather, this is Paul's charge to those who have responsibilities of building the church; and the point is, it is possible to build poorly! So let each one (Paul, Apollos, Cephas, etc.) take care *how* he builds. To have built with emphasis on human wisdom or eloquence is to have built poorly, although the minister "himself will be saved, but only as through fire" (v. 15, RSV).

Within the same context Paul then turns the figure slightly and addresses the "building" (vv. 16-17)—and this is the real point of the section. He is *not* here writing about individual Christians, and especially not about the human body (a matter which he does address in a whole new context in 6:12-20). It is the whole church whom Paul addresses. They, especially when they are assembled, are God's temple, among whom God's Spirit dwells. If anyone destroys the temple, God will destroy him! How were the

Corinthians destroying the temple? By their partisan strife which inevitably would banish the Spirit.

If this then is the correct historical exegesis of this passage (and there seems to be no other), then what about step 2; what was God's Word to the original recipients? First, there was a word to those who had "building" responsibilities, to build with care. Second, there was a word to the church, not to divide over human leaders. The church at Corinth was God's alternative to that city. To be divided was to destroy the church as God's option. Since it was in the church that God was gathering His new people and that He was now pleased to dwell, for the Corinthians to destroy that church was to put themselves under the prospect of fearful judgment.

The Hermeneutical Problems

We now come to the crux of the hermeneutical problem—step 3. What Word does I Corinthians 3:9b–17 have for us? Here the exegete insists that when there are comparable particulars in our own time, then the Word of God to us is precisely that which was spoken to the original recipients. There is still need for those with responsibilities in the church to take care how they build. It appears sadly true that the church has too often been built with wood, hay, or stubble, rather than with gold, silver, or precious stones, and such work when tried by fire has been found wanting. Furthermore, in this passage God addresses us as to our responsibilities to the local church. It must be a place where God's Spirit is known to dwell, and which therefore stands as God's alternative to the alienation, fragmentation, and loneliness of worldly society.

All of that seems easy enough. But now the real problems begin, problems for which I do not have ready answers, but for which I am prepared to suggest some directions for finding answers.

1. The Problem of Cultural Relativity

In the passage discussed above, step 3 was relatively easy because there are comparable particulars: we still have churches, which belong to God, and which have various kinds of leaders. And we still have need to assess our leaders as servants, and the leaders still need to take care how they build, and the local church still should be a place so inhabited by the Spirit that it stands as God's alternative to its pagan surroundings.

But what of those sections of the Epistles which are also clearly responses to first-century occasions, but for which we do not seem to have comparable particulars? Or to put it back one step, How does one determine what is cultural and therefore belongs only to the first century, and what is transcultural and therefore belongs to every age?[12]

These questions are not easy to answer. Let us begin by noting the obvious: some things are clearly culturally conditioned while others are just as clearly transcultural. For example, indicatives and imperatives such as, "Put on then, as God's chosen ones, holy and beloved, compassion, kindness, lowliness, meekness, and patience, forbearing one another and, if one has a complaint against another, forgiving each other" (Col. 3:12–13, RSV), clearly transcend culture. These are the "obvious" texts which seem to make the Epistles so easy to interpret.

On the other hand, for Western man the eating or noneating of food offered to idols is of no consequence. The only possible way, therefore, that we can find how I Corinthians 8–10 speaks to our situation is to go through the steps outlined above and "translate" the first-century situation into the twentieth century. The principles of

12. In all candor it should be admitted that this last question is usually answered by our own cultural predisposition. If we have been raised in a context where women pray, or prophesy, or teach, then I Timothy 2:9–15 is seen as culturally conditioned. But if our context is more strictly patriarchal, then those words are seen as transcultural and as applicable to every situation.

avoidance of acting as a stumbling block and participating in the demonic, which were God's Word to the Corinthians, are just as surely God's Word to us. *Our problem is to recognize comparable culturally-defined contexts.* Before we turn to this problem in detail, we must first examine some guidelines for determining that which is culturally relative.[13] With respect to these guidelines it should be understood that not all "obvious" things will be equally obvious to all.

a. One should first determine what is the central core of the message of the Bible and distinguish between that central core and what is dependent upon and/or peripheral to it. This is not to argue for a canon within the canon; it is to safeguard the gospel from being transformed into law through culture or religious custom.

b. Similarly, one should note whether the matter in hand is inherently moral or nonmoral, theological or nontheological. Although some may differ with my judgments here, it would appear that eating food offered to idols, a head covering for women when they pray or prophesy, women teaching in the church, and Paul's preference for celibacy are examples of issues not inherently moral; they may become so only by their use or abuse in given contexts. That is, eating *in the pagan temple* food which has been sacrificed to idols and a woman's teaching *by usurping established authority* become moral/ethical questions.

c. One must note further when the New Testament has a uniform witness on a given point and when there are differences within the New Testament itself. Thus the corporate life of the community seems to be different in Acts 2–6 and I Corinthians,[14] and one should probably not

---

13. This is a collection of some of my own material with some suggestions from my colleague, David M. Scholer. The present arrangement is my own.

14. The corporate life of the community in Acts 2–6 was not communal, but the sense of community was at a very high level. No one considered property to

make one the Word of God over against the other. More difficult here, however, are the different attitudes toward food sacrificed to idols. Compare Acts 15:29 (21:25) and Revelation 2:14, 20, on the one hand, with what Paul says in I Corinthians 8–10. Our problem here is our lack of understanding of the terminology. Did it cover all the food which had been sacrificed to idols, including that sold in the marketplace, or did it refer specifically to eating such food in the pagan temples? If the former, Paul reflects a more relaxed attitude.

d. One should be able to distinguish between principle and specific application. It is possible for a New Testament writer to support a relative application by an absolute principle and in so doing not make the application absolute. Thus in I Corinthians 11:2–16, the principle seems to be that one should do nothing to distract from the glory of God (especially by breaking convention) when the community is at worship. The specific problem seems to be relative, since Paul appeals to "custom" or "nature." Therefore, one may legitimately ask, "Would this have been an issue for us had we never encountered it in the New Testament documents?" If the specific problem were not relative, one might be tempted to argue that the culture in which any part of Scripture was given also becomes normative along with the principle itself.

e. One must keep alert to possible cultural differences between the first and twentieth centuries that are sometimes not immediately obvious. For example, to determine the role of women in the twentieth-century church, one should take into account that there were few educational opportunities for women in the first century, whereas such

be one's own private possession; rather it was made available for the whole community. In Corinth the church was composed of slaves and free (I Cor. 12:13; cf. 7:21-24). These distinctions apparently carried over to the Lord's table, where the rich went ahead with their own meals and thus humiliated those who had nothing (11:21-22). Paul says they have their own homes to eat and drink in (11:22, 34).

education is the expected norm in our society. This may affect our understanding of such texts as I Timothy 2:9–15.

f. Finally, one must exercise Christian charity at this point. Christians need to recognize the difficulties, open the lines of communication with one another, start by trying to define some principles, and have love for and a willingness to ask forgiveness from those with whom they differ.

2. The Problem of Comparable Context and Extended Application

Once one has determined that a passage is culturally relative, then he must, if he is to hear the Word of God at all, "translate" it into twentieth-century contexts in which that Word is to be heard. Very similarly, even where step 3 has comparable particulars in the twentieth century, one must ask whether that is the only context to which that Word can be addressed. Other questions inevitably arise: Are there limitations of applications? Are there principles as to what is legitimate in translating the first-century Word into a new context? Let me suggest examples of problems which arise.

a. II Corinthians 6:14—7:1 has often been used in Christian moral theology as a proof text against Christians marrying non-Christians. But neither the immediate context nor the language of the passage suggests that this is the problem Paul is addressing. Probably Calvin is right—the text in its entirety repeats the injunction of I Corinthians 10:14–22, that the Corinthians may not under any circumstances join their pagan friends at the idol's temple. Indeed, "what agreement is there between the temple of God and idols? For we are the temple of the living God." We simply have no context which is comparable. Into what kind of contexts, then, do we translate the principle, "Do not be yoked together with unbelievers"? And even if Calvin is wrong as to the particular historical context, it is surely true that this text is concerned with the community, not with individual believers. One may rightly question the legitimacy of transferring the context of this passage from the church and pagan temples to the individual Christian and his marriage.

b. I Corinthians 3:16–17, in speaking to the local church, presents the principle that what God has set aside for Himself by the indwelling of His Spirit is sacred, and whoever destroys it will come under God's awful judgment. Again, is it legitimate to apply that text to the individual Christian or to the church universal in the same way it addresses the local community of believers? Is it really legitimate to argue from this text that God will judge the believer for abusing his body? Similarly, I Corinthians 3:10–15 is addressing those with "building" responsibilities in the church, and warns of the loss they will suffer if they build poorly. Is it, then, legitimate to use this text, which speaks of judgment and salvation "as by fire," to illustrate the security of the believer?

If these are deemed legitimate applications, then the exegete would seem to have good reason to be nervous. For inherent in such "application" is the bypassing of historical exegesis. After all, to apply I Corinthians 3:16–17 to the individual believer is precisely what the church has erroneously done for centuries. Why do exegesis at all? Why not simply begin at step 3 and fall heir to centuries of error?

The exegete, therefore, would argue for two principles: (1) in translating from the first-century context to another, the two contexts must be genuinely comparable.[15] We may not all agree, of course, on our definition of the "genuinely comparable," but surely that must be the legitimizing factor. What addresses the local church speaks to the indi-

15. R. E. Brown, "Hermeneutics," uses the term *homogeneity* to express this same principle. What fails to have "homogeneity" he styles "accommodation."

vidual only as he is related to what God is saying to the whole. Therefore, it is *not* legitimate to apply I Corinthians 3:16–17 to the individual in the same way it applies to the assembly—unless he is the one destroying the assembly as God's alternative by his divisiveness! On the other hand, II Corinthians 6:14—7:1 may apply to the individual in a circuitous way, since it was as individuals that the church was "unequally yoked" to pagan temples. But even here it is better to approach the text from the standpoint of the community.

(2) Usually the "extended application" is seen to be legitimate because it is otherwise true; that is, it is clearly spelled out in other passages where it is the *intent.* If that be the case, then one should go to those other passages and stop abusing texts where it is not the intent. If there are no such passages where it is the intent, then one should ask whether that can truly be the Word of God which one learns only by "extended application."

3. The Problem of "Implication" and "Sensus Plenior"

I am here lumping together several problems which have one thing in common: Scripture is often used in such a way as to say more than was the primary intention of the human author. R. E. Brown would call these "more-than-literal" senses; but I would also include here those things that are explicit in the text, but *incidental* to the author's primary intention.

a. The exegete who is doing his work properly is forever asking the question, But what is the point? What is the author driving at? That is, he is always raising the question of the author's intent. At the same time, it is to be hoped that he is also asking questions about the content, questions of lexicology, syntax, background, and so forth. And, also, he is wary of overexegeting, for example, finding something that would stagger the author were he informed someone had found it in his writing, or building a theology upon the use of prepositions, or discovering meaning in what was *not* said.

But because he is so intent on intent, that is, finding the author's point, the exegete often comes to the text with a different agenda from that of the theologian, whose concerns are more often the content and its theological implications. An excellent case in point might be I Thessalonians 3:11: "Now may our God and Father himself, and our Lord Jesus, clear the way. . . .").

The exegete does not neglect the fact that the sentence has a compound subject and singular verb, but neither is he tempted to make too much theological hay out of it. The point is, Paul is not here trying to make a theological statement as to the unity of the Father and Son. He is concerned with returning to Thessalonica, a concern which he articulates in prayer. The exegete wants to discover why Paul shows such concern, and how that affects other things said in the epistle; he wants to know what Word there is from God to us in the wish-prayer of an apostle to a neophyte congregation in Thessalonica.

But the exegete must not, indeed dare not, overlook the theological implications of the prayer, which assumes the Father and the Son to act in unity. What is not intentionally theological is nonetheless incidentally theological; and even though it is incidental, it is not thereby unimportant, nor any less the Word of God. It is hoped the exegete and theologian differ here only in the primary interest each brings to the text.

b. What has been said above as to "extended application" continues to hold true here. What is determined to be true by implication is so on the basis of the analogy of Scripture. That is, it is either taught clearly elsewhere, or can be shown by numerous examples to be the human author's theological assumptions or presuppositions.

It is precisely for this reason that one must reject the Mormon application of I Corinthians 15:29. In spite of some exegetical gymnastics arguing for the contrary, the clear implication of that text is that some Corinthians were practicing baptism for the dead. I am of the mind that it is also implied in the text that Paul is not terribly shaken by the practice. But the analogy of Scripture scarcely allows us to regard such a practice as either mandatory or repeatable by later Christians. For neither by implication nor by explication do we have the faintest idea as to the particulars of that baptism—for whom, by whom, for what reasons, and with what significance. Here is a place where the point of the text is clear: in a purely *ad hoc* argument, Paul says that the practice argues for a future resurrection; otherwise what these Corinthians are doing is absurd. But what in fact they were doing remains a singular mystery belonging to first-century Corinth.

c. A final point here. The apparent identification of Jesus with the Spirit in II Corinthians 3:17 ("Now the Lord is the Spirit") has long been a *crux interpretum* for exegetes and theologians. Along with I Corinthians 15:45 this passage seems to lend credence to a kind of Spirit Christology, as if for Paul the risen Lord and the Spirit are one and the same (so Hans Lietzmann). But as a matter of fact, what seems to be implied rather strongly is *not* said by Paul at all. The point is, sound exegesis will often correct erroneous inferences, and such inferences must always be subject to exegesis.

In the passage at hand, Paul has been glorying in his privilege of ministry in the new covenant, a covenant brought on by the coming of the Spirit and contrasted with the covenant of the letter, which led to death. To illustrate the greater glory of this new covenant he inserts a *pesher* (a special kind of Jewish commentary) of Exodus 34:29–34. He concludes by citing Exodus 34:34, with slight changes so as to move it from Moses to the present. Thus, "whenever anyone [not Moses only] turns to the Lord, 'the veil is taken away'" (II Cor. 3:16, NIV). Now "the Lord" being referred to in this passage, Paul goes on to say, is the Spirit, the life-giving Spirit of the new covenant; and where the Spirit of the Lord is, there is liberty (=the freedom of the new covenant, freedom from the law with its imposition of death). The passage, therefore, is a pneumatological one, not Christological, and is not identifying Christ and the Spirit even by implication.

But is it not possible that there is a *sensus plenior,* a deeper or secondary meaning to such texts? After all, taken by itself, II Corinthians 3:17 does use language to identify Christ with the Spirit. Is it not possible that God intended something quite beyond what the human author intended? Besides, we have the example of the New Testament writers, who, in exegeting the Old Testament, found *sensus plenior.* Is it not possible on such grounds that those people are right who argue that "the perfect" in I Corinthians 13:10 does indeed mean the canon?

Some observations and personal opinions: (1) There is inherent danger in the concept of *sensus plenior.* If indeed God intends something beyond what the human author intended—and I would certainly not deny that possibility—then who speaks for God? That is, who determines the deeper meaning God intends for us? The magisterium? The Dispensationalist's view of history? I admit to being squeamish regarding the whole idea.

(2) The fact that the New Testament writers found *sensus plenior* in the Old Testament does not help me much. R. N. Longenecker has argued, and I tend to agree, that we cannot repeat the exegesis of the New Testament writers, precisely because what they did at that point was inspired.[16] In this case we know God's fuller meaning in the Old Testament because He revealed it to the New Testament writers. But this can scarcely serve as a model for the twentieth century, any more than Paul's use of *pesher* and allegory can.

---

16. Most recently in *Biblical Exegesis in the Apostolic Period* (Grand Rapids: Wm. B. Eerdmans, 1975), especially pp. 205–20.

(3) There is for me the possibility of a *sensus plenior* in predictive prophecy. But if so, it would seem to be something available to us only after the fact, not before. Therefore, I would tend to hold such interpretations in abeyance.

(4) All of this leads me to suggest that a *sensus plenior* in the Epistles is not a solid option, except perhaps where the writer is engaging in predictive prophecy.

Some Concluding Remarks

How, then, is all of this concern for greater precision in the exegesis and hermeneutics of the Epistles related to the battle of inerrancy? In several ways, I think.

1. Even if one is uncomfortable with my special use of the terms, the distinction I have made between exegesis and hermeneutics is a very important one. The first task of the interpreter is to discover what the text *meant* when it was originally written. The question of the inerrancy and trustworthiness of Scripture *must* be carried on at that level, *not* at the level of "what does the text mean for us today." This is not a way of trying to get around anything. In fact a careful reading of this paper will indicate that quite the opposite is my intent. All of Scripture is God's Word. The hermeneutical task is to free that Word to speak to our own situation.

My point here is a crucial one. We simply must be done with the nonsense that suggests that some evangelicals are "soft on Scripture" because, for example, they believe in women's ministries in the church. One may as well accuse B. B. Warfield of not believing in inerrancy because he had a hermeneutical way to get around Paul's very clear command to seek spiritual gifts, especially prophecy. The so-called women's issue is a hermeneutical question, and we will have differences here. But those differences are not questions of the authority of Scripture. They are questions of interpretation, and have to do with our historical distance from the text and the whole question of cultural relativity. We will not all agree on the principles I have suggested. But surely we must agree that hermeneutics is the arena in which we must carry on the discussion, not in the arena of the doctrine of Scripture per se.

2. If the battle of inerrancy must be carried on at the exegetical level—and it must—then we simply cannot afford to play loose with the text at that point. Here is one of the great weaknesses in Harold Lindsell's book, for example. Through a series of contrived interpretations he does things to the biblical text that good exegetical method must stand against.

A case in point. In order to reconcile some apparent difficulties between the Synoptic and Johannine accounts of Peter's denials, Lindsell argues that Peter really denied Jesus six times! It may be argued, by sheer sophistry, that for the biblical writers to say *three* does not exclude the possibility of six, because six can also include any number up to six. But that is to play havoc with the clear intent of the biblical writers who clearly say that there would be *three* denials. To turn that three into six by a kind of hermeneutical harmony in the fashion of Tatian's heretical *Diatessaron* borders on arguing *for* an errant text. I remember a day in 1975 when Fred Lynn of the Boston Red Sox batted in ten runs in a single game. Had a reporter for the Boston *Globe* written that Lynn batted in five runs, the reporter would not technically have been in error, for Lynn did in fact bat in five runs. But not a person in Boston who saw the game would have been convinced that the sportswriter was not really in error. For the clear intent of such reporting is not to give part of the whole, but the whole itself.

Furthermore, to say that God really meant six when the Word clearly says three seems to contravene the nature of God and His revelation. It is to argue that God intended to obfuscate rather than to reveal or make plain. Exegesis, therefore, must be carried on with precision.

3. Since inerrancy must be wrestled with at the exegetical level, the real question in the debate is *not* so-called limited inerrancy. Rather it has to do with the amount of accommodation one believes the Holy Spirit allowed the human authors.

That there is *some* accommodation one can scarcely deny. The very fact that God chose to give His Word in ordinary human language, through real people, in real historical settings, is an expression of this accommodation.

Thus, the Bible is not just a collection of sayings or propositions from God, written in a unique, divine language. God did not say, "Learn these truths: Number 1. There is no God but one, and I am He. Number 2. I am the creator of all things, including mankind." And so on. These propositions are indeed true, and they are found in the Bible. A collection of such propositions might have made things easier for us, to be sure! But God chose to speak His Word through a wide range of literary forms (narrative histories, chronicles, law codes, dramas, all kinds of poems, proverbs, prophetic oracles, parables, stories, letters, Gospels, and apocalypses). Each of these is a different kind of human speech, and each requires its own special rules for interpretation.

There is also a wide range of people who were used by the Holy Spirit to write Scripture. Thus we can distinguish between the way Paul and John express themselves theologically as well as between their grammar and literary style. To say they differ in expression is not to say that they are opposed, or that one of them is in error.

Another expression of accommodation is to be found in the fourfold Gospel. People like Tatian and some well-meaning modern authors have always been embarrassed by that reality and attempt to harmonize the four into one. But it was God who inspired the four. We do well to keep it that way. The fact that the Aramaic words that Jesus originally spoke are now recorded for us in Greek translation is already an accommodation. So also is the fact that His words as they are recorded in one Gospel are not usually duplicated exactly in the others.

Such expressions of accommodation are accepted by all evangelicals, and even by some fundamentalists. The *real* problem here is, where do we draw the line? *The differences that exist among evangelicals are basically a matter of finding a starting point.* Do we start with a theological a priori and say what God *must* do, or do we start with the text itself and say what God *did* do? As an exegete my sympathies obviously lie with the latter option.

Take, for example, the question of whether accommodation allows for the human author to speak popularly, even if such speech is not precise according to modern scientific norms. The exegete sees Jesus speaking popularly in Matthew 13:32 when He says that the mustard seed "is the smallest of all your seeds" (NIV). But if one argues a priori that every botanical allusion in Scripture must carry the precision of the twentieth-century botanist, then he must resort once again to remote possibilities that are improbable in the highest degree.[17]

I do not wish to resolve this issue here, for that would require a paper of much greater length. However, these are the kinds of questions that must form *a part of the discussion;* and no philosophical or emotional a priori should be allowed to prejudge how the believer in biblical inerrancy *must* decide these questions.

4. Finally, I will contend for one thing above all. The *occasional* nature of the New Testament Epistles is scarcely debatable. This does indeed give us many and varied exegetical and hermeneutical problems. But the fact that they are occasional is also their greater glory! Instead of trying to circumvent that reality by a variety of hermeneutical ploys, we should affirm with thanksgiving that the

---

17. On this issue Lindsell allows for the possibility of accommodation (*Battle for the Bible,* p. 169), but it also seems clear that he would prefer not to have to make this allowance.

weakness of God is stronger than men and the foolishness of God is wiser than men. The same God who spoke His living Word most eloquently through the weakness of an incarnation, has also spoken His written Word through the weakness of human language and human history. That this Word was so spoken *once* is precisely what gives us the courage to believe it will so speak again and again despite the relativities and ambiguities of history. The Eternal Word never changes, even though the historical circumstances in which it speaks are ever subject to change.

JAMES I. PACKER

8

Preaching as Biblical Interpretation

This essay seeks to explore the thesis that, the Bible being what it is, all true interpretation of it must take the form of preaching. With this goes an equally important converse: that, preaching being what it is, all true preaching must take the form of biblical interpretation. The basis for the former thesis is that Scripture is the God-given record, explanation, and application of God's once-for-all redemptive words and deeds on the stage of space-time history, and that its intended function is to "instruct . . . for salvation through faith in Christ Jesus" (II Tim. 3:15). To give this instruction is precisely, in the biblical sense of the word, to preach. The basis for the latter thesis is that preaching means speaking God's own message in His name, that is, as His representative, and this is possible for fallen men, with their sin-twisted minds, only as they labor faithfully to echo, restate, and reapply God's once-for-all witness to Himself, which, as we said, is the sum and substance of Holy Scripture.

Current debate about the veracity of particular biblical

statements tends to lose sight of the fact that God in His providence gave us the Bible not to be a sort of encyclopedia catering to curiosity ("Everyman's *Enquire Within Upon Everything*"), not to be a means of increasing historical knowledge for its own sake, but to introduce us to the living, speaking God who made us, and to the crucified, risen, reigning, and returning Christ, man's Redeemer, and in so doing to show us all what we should believe and do and hope for as we travel home to God through this present world. It is because this is so that preaching must be seen as the paradigmatic way of handling the Bible; and no method of studying it, however erudite and formally orthodox, can be approved further than it embodies the preacher's kerygmatic perspective and purpose.

The maxim that exegesis and biblical interpretation are for the sake of an adequate systematic theology is true, yet if one stops there one has told only half the story. The other half, the complementary truth which alone can ward off the baleful misunderstanding that a particular rational orthodoxy is all that matters, is that the main reason for seeking an adequate systematic theology is for the sake of better and more profound biblical interpretation. Calvin's *Institutio* is a classic of systematic theology, yet in the Preface to the second and later editions he described it as a propaedeutic for biblical interpretation;[1] and interpretation means theological exegesis of the text, in relation to the rest of the organism of revealed truth, plus reapplication of what it yields for our illumination and reformation—in other words, for the scripturally defined purposes of teaching, reproof, correction, and training in righteousness (cf. II Tim. 3:16). But this is, precisely, preaching. In always identifying himself as, by calling, a preacher of the Word, Calvin showed that he understood his own logic very well. Those who, like myself, are called to teach systematic theology need often to ponder the same point.

---

1. *Corpus Reformatorum,* vol. I, pp. 255f.; or *Institutes of the Christian Religion,* trans. F. L. Battles (Philadelphia: Westminster Press, 1970), p. 7.

Preaching and the Bible

The basic reason why biblical interpretation must take the form of preaching is that the Bible itself is preaching. What is preaching? Teaching, and more; not just shoveling information into the head, but appealing to the heart, to the whole man; as one declares truths in God's name, he calls on God's behalf for a response of faith, obedience, and worship. Here is the essential difference between sermons, acts of preaching, and mere lectures. The main New Testament words for preaching are κηρύσσω, meaning to make a public announcement as a herald (κῆρυξ) does, and εὐαγγελίζομαι, meaning to impart the good news, the gospel (εὐαγγέλιον). The scope of preaching as an activity is shown in II Corinthians 5:20—6:1: "We are ambassadors for Christ, God making his appeal through us. We beseech you on behalf of Christ, be reconciled to God. . . . Working together with him . . . we entreat you not to accept the grace of God [i.e., the message about it] in vain" (RSV). Such poignant appeal for response, expressing not only the messenger's personal concern for the welfare of his fellow men but also the compassion of the God whose ambassador he is, has always been integral to true preaching (cf. Deut. 30:15-20; Ezek. 18:23, 32; 33:11; Hos. 14; Jon. 3-4). Preaching appears in the Bible as a relaying of what God has said about Himself and His doings, and about men in relation to Him, plus a pressing of His commands, promises, warnings, and assurances, with a view to winning the hearer or hearers (or, if it is being done by writing, the readers) to a positive response. So it is a mistake to define preaching institutionally, in terms of buildings, pulpits, pews, and stated services, however true it is that preaching has been institutionalized among us in these terms. But preaching should in the first instance be defined functionally, as an activity of communication, whether by monologue or in dialogue, whether to a group or to one person only (as when Philip "preached . . . Jesus" to the Ethiopian eunuch [Acts 8:35, KJV], or when Jesus preached to the woman at the well [John 4]), which has in view the evoking of a positive response to some aspect of God's call to men.

If, now, we apply this definition to the Bible itself, we soon perceive that all sixty-six books are, directly or indirectly, preaching. In their character as God's mouthpieces the prophets proclaim, and subsequently write, messages of divine appeal to Israel. In their role as Christ's agents and ambassadors, the apostles write words of exhortation, epistolary sermons, to Christians. The Old Testament historians, whom the Jews perceptively called the former prophets, narrate God's dealings with men and nations in a way that is clearly meant to evoke praise and teach lessons about faith and unbelief that will mold their readers' lives. The Gospels prove on inspection to be, not artless memoirs of Jesus, as was once thought, but four careful selections of stories about His sayings, doings, and sufferings, all carefully arranged and angled so that "the gospel"—the good news of Jesus, inviting faith in Him—leaps out into the thoughtful reader's mind. The wisdom literature, of which it was well said that the Psalms teach us how to praise, the Proverbs how to live, the Song how to love, Job how to endure, and Ecclesiastes how to enjoy, is didactic preaching in substance if not in literary form. So we might go on. When Paul says that "whatever was written in former days was written for our instruction, that . . . by the encouragement of the scriptures we might have hope" (Rom. 15:4, RSV), his thought is that God's intention in causing the Old Testament books to be set down included their functioning in due course as His own preaching to Christians. So these books are not human preaching only, but God's preaching too. Indeed, there is no truer or happier way to describe the Scriptures of both Testaments, in their once-for-all God-givenness and present dynamism, than as *God preaching.* Their inspiration, in the sense of divine origin and authenticity as expressions of God's mind, and their instrumentality as God's means of addressing mankind today, are both comprehended in this phrase.

Two things follow. First, since divine-human preaching is its nature, it is only as divine-human preaching that Scripture can be understood, and that is tantamount to saying that it will be understood only through actual preaching of it. It is the special merit of Gustaf Wingren's book, *The Living Word,*[2] to follow Luther in emphasizing this. Only as we hear the biblical message preached and applied to us, and as we preach and apply it ourselves in our private meditations, and as (to adopt a phrase from John Owen) it "preaches itself in our own souls,"[3] do we come to appreciate what its real burden is. Apart from this, the most we can have is correct notions about the message, but correct notions do not constitute spiritual understanding. It is the work of the Holy Spirit in and through preaching to cause that which is God's Word in itself to be understood and received as God's message to ourselves, and its contents to be apprehended as direct communication to us from heaven. Where there is no such preaching there will be no such understanding, no matter how carefully Scripture is studied and explored from a historical standpoint. This explains how it is possible for highly motivated students even in evangelical seminaries to find that the effect of their technically disciplined biblical studies is to make Scripture seem more remote and less alive than before; if they are not constantly exposed to applicatory preaching, preaching which constantly discloses to them the character of Scripture as both the content and the means of God's communication with us here and now, this can very easily happen. If it does, however, the fault is not, as obscurantist reaction sometimes urges,

2. Gustaf Wingren, *The Living Word* (Philadelphia: Muhlenberg Press, 1960).
3. John Owen, *The True Nature of a Gospel Church* in *Works,* ed. W. H. Goold (Edinburgh: T. & T. Clark, 1862), vol. 16, p. 76.

in technical Bible study, but in the lack of true preaching within the student's personal milieu.

Second, the Bible must itself preach in our preaching. It is not for us to speak on the Bible's behalf, but to let the Bible speak for itself through us. "Preach the word," said Paul (II Tim. 4:2); he did not say, preach about the Word. The Westminster Directory for Public Worship rightly required preachers, when raising a point from a text, to labor to let their hearers see "how God teacheth it from thence"[4]—in other words, to demonstrate that the point is being read out of the text, not read into it. This is the true prophetic element in preaching: as biblical prophets mediated God by relaying His Word as they found it in their hearts, so Christian preachers are to mediate God by relaying His Word as it meets them in their texts. The Puritans, like many since, spoke of preaching, in echo of Luke 24:32, as "opening" or "opening up" the Scriptures, as one opens up a previously locked house or garden. The image is suggestive: through the opened entry you see in and can be led in, and the owner may come out to meet you himself. So with Scripture: as it is "opened" in preaching, you see glories that are new, and find yourself in fellowship with God. But this can happen only where the preacher's purpose and strategy are to serve the text and let Scripture itself speak.

Preaching the Bible

The preacher's task, as we have said, is biblical interpretation—which means not just historical exegesis,

4. *The Directory for the Public Worship of God* states: "In raising doctrines from the text, [the preacher's] care ought to be, *First,* That the matter be the truth of God. *Secondly,* That it be a truth contained in or grounded on that text, that the hearers may discern how God teacheth it from thence" (*The Confession of Faith. . .*, issued by the Publications Committee of the Free Presbyterian Church of Scotland, 1967, p. 379).

but application too. The Bible is an ancient library; it consists of sixty-six books, written at different times from just under two to rather more than three millennia ago. Biblical interpretation is the art of so reading and explaining these old books that they become—or rather, are seen to be, for in themselves they always were—relevant to the modern reader. That is a formal definition; its material counterpart would be, the act of so elucidating these books that God's personally-directed message is discerned in them and His presence as He speaks to us is thereby realized. Schleiermacher and his followers, seeing Scripture as essentially a transcript of religious feeling by the use of appropriate conceptual imagery (a view strikingly parallel to Wordsworth's definition of poetry as emotion recollected in tranquility), understood the interpretive process empathetically, in terms of readers' "tuning in" to the feelings expressed; the neoorthodox, seeing Scripture as essentially a human word of witness which by grace becomes God's means of addressing us, understood the interpretive process dynamically and dialogically, in terms of identifying with and directing to our own situation the outlook of biblical men who, under God's promise and command, humbly listened for His word of judgment and mercy. An adequate view of biblical interpretation will start by asserting what both liberals and neoorthodox deny, namely, that the sixty-six books are inspired in the sense that God is their ultimate author, so that all their affirmations must be received as God-taught truth; but beyond this it will embrace the positive thrusts of both positions. The profile of such a view may be sketched in as follows:

1. Models

The neoorthodox insistence that biblical interpretation is first and foremost a matter of learning to listen to the living God, and letting Him interpret us, is right. There are two models or analogies whereby we may picture the process.

The first model is the *tutorial.* In a British university, a tutor may meet with a group of students for an hour's instruction in a subject on which one of the group has written an essay. The tutor may ask him to read his essay and then, as an alternative to inviting class discussion, criticize it directly, while the rest of the group listen and learn from the exchange. If the tutor does his job well, they will soon see what he would think of the ideas they might bring to the class, and where those ideas would in fact need amplifying and amending. Similarly, interpreters of Scripture go to school, as it were, with men of Bible times, Noah, Abraham, David, Peter, the Jews at various periods in their history, the Christians at Corinth, at Thessalonica, at Laodicea, and so on. We overhear God dealing with these people, encouraging, correcting, instructing; thus we learn His thoughts about our thoughts, and His purposes for and ways with our lives. Now God has appointed preaching as a means to enable His church to learn of Him in this way.

The second, complementary model is *coaching.* If you have ever been coached in any sport, you know how the coach breaks up the even tenor of playing habits that have come to seem natural, and insists that in order to do it right (a golf swing, or a tennis shot, or whatever) you must learn to do it differently, in a way which at first you find unnatural and difficult. Similarly, as interpreters of Scripture we find ourselves confronted with God the coach, who insists on teaching us how to live, forcing us to break bad habits which seem natural and to learn new ones which at first seem hard. Often the discipline is felt to be irksome, but the profit of accepting it is untold. God has appointed preaching as a means of drawing His people into acceptance of His discipline for their lives.

Current reflection on the interpreting of Scripture stresses the need to take account of cultural differences between the various eras from which the biblical books come, and rightly insists that these differences run very deep. When exponents of the so-called new hermeneutic dwell on the traumatic effect of having biblical "horizons," or perspectives, intersect with and challenge our own, those horizons which belong to us as cultural and religious children of our own time, they do well. We are all of us more limited and provincial, culturally speaking, than we ever succeed in realizing, and on this account are in constant danger of mishearing, misconstruing, or simply disregarding biblical instruction; therefore, the insistence of the new hermeneutic that we must self-consciously "distance" the horizons of our contemporary outlook(s) from those of the biblical outlook(s) before we attempt to "fuse" them, should be heeded. We may not domesticate the Bible by slotting it directly into our world and forgetting how far a cry it is from the late twentieth-century West to the biblical period in the Near East; we shall miss a great deal of the Bible's meaning and challenge if we do. Yet, granted all that, there is need to balance this emphasis on the relativities of culture by stressing that some things do not change, even when cultural forms do. The Triune God, to start with, remains the same; so, at bottom, does fallen human nature; so do the law and the gospel; so do repentance, faith, joy, praise, love to God and neighbor, and all the other qualities which make up godliness; so do the demonic dynamics that animate godless society; so do God's covenant relation with His people, and His saving grace in Christ. Our two models assume these and related continuities. The assumption seems a safe one, and we shall not apologize for making it, nor for insisting that preaching which is authentically biblical will certainly embody it.

2. Materials

What is the Bible, this composite of sixty-six books that we are to interpret, really all about? All ventures in interpretation imply some answer to this question, and interpretations vary according to the answer that is assumed. All interpretation reflects our personal interest, or preoccupation, or blinkers (put it as you wish). Thus, if ancient history or the history of religions is our interest, our biblical interpretation will focus on that; if our concern is with theological truth, or religious experience, or the ways of the living God, our interpretation will reflect that too. Similarly, if our approach to Christianity is shaped by an uncriticized individualism, we are likely to overlook the Bible's corporate and churchly perspective; if it is shaped by antiintellectualism in any form, we shall probably miss the Bible's challenge to our minds.

Every theology has its built-in hermeneutic, and every hermeneutic is implicitly a total theology. Theology in the tradition of Luther sees Scripture as essentially law and gospel; theology in the tradition of Calvin reads the Bible as essentially God's declaration of His covenant; theology in the tradition of Schleiermacher views what is written as the verbalizing of a felt affinity with God; theology in the tradition of Barth construes the Bible as witness to the God-man Jesus Christ, who (so Barth held) is the sum and substance of all our knowledge both of God and of ourselves; and so on. Wise interpreters will accept enrichment from all these hermeneutical approaches, and more besides, but their final goal will be to let the Bible, as God's own preaching, speak for itself and shape their interest to itself. And, doing that, they will find that it is *both* a complex proclamation and celebration of God's saving plan and action in Christ *and* a book of life, exhibiting in a multitude of particular cases what human relationships with the living God really involve. It is *both* a declaring of redemptive revelation *and* a demonstration of believing response to it; *both* an interpretative history of those unique events whereby God has created a people for Himself through Jesus Christ *and* a spelling out of the universal relevance of these events for every man in every age; *both* an announcement that the living God has come to us in

Christ, *and* a consequent summons to mankind to come through Christ to God, with promises and commands showing how, individually and in our various communal relationships, He is to be served. Thus attentive interpreters will understand the Bible, and thus they will preach it.

3. Method

A full-scale discussion of how Scripture can be successfully interpreted would require, on the one hand, a good deal of paradigmatic analysis of what the sixty-six books contain and, on the other, some sustained reflection on the conditions of theological and spiritual understanding—a field in which Luther's dictum that prayer, meditation, and temptation (*oratio, meditatio, tentatio*) make the theologian remains the best starting point.[5] Here, however, we can attempt neither of these things, and must limit ourselves to laying down three procedural principles which are basic conditions of success, in the sense that any violation of them is of itself, immediately and inescapably, a failure in the interpretative task.

a. *Hold to the literal meaning.* "Literal" here is defined as the meaning which the human writer, inspired as he was, has actually expressed in the words that he has chosen to use. To call this method "literal" is to follow sixteenth-century usage, and to echo the Reformers' antithesis against "allegorical" interpretation, which reads into biblical passages meanings that cannot be read out of them because they were not demonstrably in the author's mind. The "literal" sense is thus the "natural," "historical" sense, the sense that each author, as a responsible communicator, was concerned to convey, and that the persons to whom each book was first addressed should have gathered from the words he had written. The "literal" method is thus the

5. "Preface to the Wittenberg Edition of Luther's German Writings, 1539," in *Luther's Works,* American edition (Philadelphia: Muhlenberg Press, 1960), vol. 34, p. 285. Cf. Weimar Ausgabe, vol. 50, p. 659.

"grammatico-historical" method of Reformation and post-Reformation exegesis, in which linguistic usage, historical background, cultural presuppositions, and conventions of communication in each writer's own day are allowed to be decisive for determining what each document means.

There is, to be sure, a sense in which Old Testament writers constantly express and communicate to Christian readers more than they themselves knew, for Christians read the Old Testament in the light of New Testament knowledge of the fulfilling of types and prophecies, and of the further unfolding of God's plan for world history, through our Lord Jesus Christ; thus realities which were opaque to the prophets (cf. I Peter 1:10–12) are clear to Christians, and Old Testament foreshadowings of them are correspondingly more meaningful to Christians than they could be to their original authors. But such enhanced meanings simply extrapolate from the expressed meaning, in the light of God's unfolded plan, and do not in any way involve the element of arbitrariness and flight from the literal sense, which was the vice of medieval allegory.

There is also a sense in which every New Testament writer communicates to Christians today more than he knew he was communicating, simply because Christians can now read his work as part of the completed New Testament canon. Each book by each writer gains new significance in this larger context, where comparisons and cross-references can be made; and each book is constantly found both to supplement, and to be supplemented by, others. But in each case it is, precisely, the literal sense that gains significance, not any other sense. Indeed, there is no other!—for the whole point of the doctrine of inspiration is that thereby man's word and God's Word have become one, so that the human literal sense is in truth God's message, and the way into God's mind is via the human author's expressed meaning.

b. *Hold to the principle of harmony.* Inspiration, as was

said, is God's work of so determining men's testimony to Him that their witness becomes identical with His own instruction to us. The basic theological significance of calling Scripture "inerrant" is as an avowal of this identity, for if all that the human authors affirm is also affirmed by God, it must follow that whatever they have affirmed is true. It is a pity that the association of "inerrant" in some minds, and indeed in some circles, with unnatural and invalid exegesis of Scripture discourages some from using the word to make this point, for the point needs making and "inerrant" makes it neatly. Only assertions of inspiration which entail inerrancy are assertions of that inspiration, that total identity of human and divine witness, of which Scripture speaks.

But if all that the biblical writers affirm should be taken as true, it can never be right to posit a real and substantial contradiction between one biblical statement and another, nor to suppose that where biblical statement and secular information appear to conflict the Bible may be wrong. We may of course have misunderstood the biblical passages in question (when discrepancies appear, we should check our exegesis and see), but as a matter of intellectual method we should hold fast to the certainty that their genuine meaning, if we can determine it, is true, because they are inspired. So in all our biblical interpretation we should use the concept of inerrancy as a control, and seek to exhibit the harmony of Scripture both with itself and with secular information whenever questions of consistency arise. We should not be so mesmerized by these questions that we think of nothing else, but equally we should not evade them when they come up. And should it happen that for the present we can find no harmonistic hypothesis that seems sufficiently cogent, we should choose to wait for one to appear, and be willing temporarily not to know the answer, rather than be stampeded into joining those who in one way or another accuse particular biblical passages of theological or empirical falsehood.

c. *Follow round the interpretative spirals.* By "interpretative spirals" I mean three particular mental procedures whereby understanding of particular elements in the biblical revelation may be constantly refined and deepened. I speak of "spirals" because in each case we return to the point from which we set out, but higher up, so to speak, because now we see more of what we are looking at. Anyone who has traveled round the successive loops of an ascending spiral on a railroad (in Switzerland, for instance, or India or New Zealand) will take my meaning. It appears to me that in any preaching ministry in which the Bible is regularly being interpreted to the same congregation, constant traveling upward round these interpretative spirals is of very great importance.

The first upward spiral concerns *the exploration of the Bible from within.*

If you want to take the measure of the mind of a versatile and prolific teacher, such as Karl Barth, or C. S. Lewis, or to get a proper understanding of some period of history, or some major philosophical debate, you will have to read a series of books—books by the teacher, books about the period, books bearing on the problem. These books will often comprise more than one literary form. The more you read, the more deeply you will understand each new item, for your overall acquaintance with the field is becoming more adequate, and both your discernment and your judgment are ripening. But in due course you will need to go back and reread the items you read first, and link them up with your maturer understanding, for at first reading you were only a beginner and so could not help missing much of their significance.

So with our progressive grasp of the contents of Scripture. The Bible is an organism of revealed truth, to which all sixty-six books contribute in various ways. Within this organism are internal links of several kinds—for example, thematic links (e.g., such themes as God, godliness, church, covenant, atonement, salvation, God's kingdom, the Messiah, judgment, prayer); links of parallel subject matter (e.g., Kings and Chronicles, the four Gospels, Ephesians and Colossians); links of typology (e.g., Leviticus and Hebrews) and fulfilled prophecy (e.g., Isaiah and the Gospels); and links of common authorship (e.g., the works of Paul, Luke, Peter, John, and, if one dare say it, Moses). Preaching must constantly explore these links, elucidating the relation of the different ingredients in the Bible to each other, so that our sight of the total biblical landscape may, so to speak, spiral up, becoming progressively more adequate.

The second upward spiral concerns *the intersecting of biblical horizons with our own.*

I say "horizons" rather than "perspectives" or "viewpoints" because that word suggests the *limits* of a field of vision, and it is a point about limits that I wish to make. The spiritual horizons of professed Christian people are always more limited than they should be, sometimes scandalously so, and our sense of reality is always more or less defective as a result. Unconsciously we are man-centered, self-centered, self-sufficient, self-confident; we think about our living in ways which magnify man and diminish God; we appear as individualists not concerned enough about community, or as churchmen with a social conscience not concerned enough about individuals, or as pietists so heavenly-minded as to be of no earthly use, or as pragmatists so materially- and managerially-minded that our hearts are entirely earthbound. Also, as children of our age (which we all are, however much we wish we weren't and perhaps claim not to be), we have our horizons narrowed by any number of conventional prejudices, assumptions, and insensitivities. The Bible's point of view must constantly be brought to challenge and correct these limited horizons of our own present vision. Thus, for instance, we shall need again and again to be faced with the double reality of our creation in God's image (which shows us our true dignity and destiny) and our constant moral perversity at the motivational level (which shows us our real wretchedness and disgrace apart from Jesus Christ). We shall need from time to time to relearn the doctrine of justification by faith not only as a counter to the paralysis of past guilt but also as God's support for living with the knowledge of present failure. We may need too to learn and relearn its Christ-centered, God-honoring thrust, and to be weaned away by it from the bondage of pious self-observation. Or we may need to be corrected and challenged ethically regarding areas of liberty where we have not behaved responsibly and areas of responsibility where we have hitherto behaved frivolously.

These random examples illustrate the kind of encounter between God's Word and our ways which preaching must constantly aim to bring about. Through such encounters our horizons may be enlarged and refocused, and under such judgments from the Word our understanding will be increased. This is edification. And because the channels in our hearts along which spiritual awareness and conviction flow tend constantly to silt up, the same lessons will need to be preached to us over and over again. Thus our insight under God may grow, as through preaching basic challenges recur, spiraling up in repetitions of the old lessons with ever more searching and far-reaching applications.

The third upward spiral concerns *the growth of self-knowledge through knowledge of God.*

Just about all our wisdom, said Calvin in the famous opening sentence of his *Institutio,* consists in knowing God and knowing ourselves; and the process begins with knowing God.[6] It was when Isaiah in the temple "saw the Lord" and heard the angels celebrate His holiness that he came to know himself as unclean in God's sight, and to experience God's pardon existentially. The shape of the spiral here is that the more clearly we see God's transcendent power, holiness, and glory, the more clearly we shall be made

---

6. John Calvin, *Institutes of the Christian Religion,* I.i.1.

aware of our weakness, sinfulness, and utter need; our helplessness will drive us back to God in that self-distrust which is basic to faith in Him and thereby we shall come to appreciate His glory the more as His mercy touches our needs. It is the task of preaching to insure that our sense of God's glory should spiral up constantly as the realities of His judgment and mercy touch us in ever deeper and more probing ways.

The Bible Preaching

Preachers whose beliefs about biblical inspiration and inerrancy vacillate can hardly avoid trying from time to time to guard against supposedly unworthy thoughts which the Bible, if believed as it stands, might engender. This presumptuous procedure, at once comic and pathetic, will not, however, mark the preacher who receives the Bible as God's teaching and testimony. His aim, rather, will be to stand under Scripture, not over it, and to allow it, so to speak, to talk through him, delivering what is not so much his message as its. In our preaching, this is what should always be happening. In his obituary of the great German conductor, Otto Klemperer, Neville Cardus spoke of the way in which Klemperer "set the music in motion," maintaining throughout a deliberately anonymous, self-effacing style in order that the musical notes might articulate themselves in their own integrity through him. So it must be in preaching; Scripture itself must do all the talking, and the preacher's task is simply to "set the Bible in motion." Happy are those hearers to whom the Bible—that is, God in and through the Bible—talks in this way, through the lips of preachers who honor the Bible as God's true Word and whose purpose is simply and solely to be its servant.